HURTS GIVEN AND RECEIVED

·

SLOWLY

Howard Barker

HURTS GIVEN AND RECEIVED

•

SLOWLY

OBERON BOOKS
LONDON

First published in 2010 by Oberon Books Ltd
521 Caledonian Road, London N7 9RH
Tel: 020 7607 3637 / Fax: 020 7607 3629
e-mail: info@oberonbooks.com
www.oberonbooks.com

A catalogue record for this book is available from the British
Library.

ISBN: 978-1-84943-016-6

Cover Image by Eduardo Houth

Printed in Great Britain by CPI Antony Rowe, Chippenham.

Contents

HURTS GIVEN AND RECEIVED

DURING THE MAKING OF A WORK OF ART
REVILED AND SUBSEQUENTLY REVERED

Characters

BACH	A Proprietor
ALWAYS	An Aged Servant
FELLTRAY	A Mistress to Bach
DETRIMENT	A Friend to Bach
GLOVE	The Mother of Detriment
RIB	An Undertaker
UMBER	" "
ALZARIN	" "
SADOVEE	A Schoolgirl
SEPTEMBER	A Female Police Officer
MCNOY	A Brutal Man and a Father
SADOVEE TWO	Twin Sister to Sadovee
OBLAST	A Visitor
BOLLY	" "
HAYDN	" "
STAYS	" "
TABLET	" "
GNATCH	" "
BULOW	" "

1

A man seated at a high desk, inscribing. An older man enters, frowning and afraid.

ALWAYS: Master / I'm ill /

    (His appearance goes unremarked.)

    Master /

BACH: *(Without lifting his eyes.)* I heard you /

    (BACH writes. He descends from his stool and leaves the room. The older man shrinks, decays. BACH returns with a book, and resumes his work. In the silence, the sound of his pen.)

ALWAYS: Master / I'm ill /

    (The pen. The creak of the high stool. ALWAYS goes to leave, his movements pained.)

BACH: This illness /

    (He does not lift his eyes from the page.)

    The severity of which entitles you to march into my study to announce it / this illness restricts your capacity for labour / I daresay / is that a sufficient reason / I ask myself / why it should also restrict mine? /

    (At last BACH lifts his eyes to ALWAYS.)

    Find some shade / lie down / drink vinegar / nine parts vinegar / to one part wine /

ALWAYS: Master / I'm dying /

    (BACH studies the old man. He closes his book.)

BACH: Go home then / go home to die /

    (ALWAYS turns to leave.)

And put your tools away / it does not matter that they are not cleaned / just hang them on their hooks / if tools are left about they are invariably stolen /

(ALWAYS shuffles away. BACH returns to his page.)

You have been loyal / and scrupulous / and honest / both to my father / and to me /

(ALWAYS limps on, and stops.)

ALWAYS: Master /

(He is hesitant.)

My wife / my old wife / she /

BACH: When I commended your long service I did not expect to be importuned for favours / please do not embarrass me by asking for what you know cannot be granted / she must surrender the tenancy in the normal way / one week and one day / after your death /

(ALWAYS suffers.)

ALWAYS: I wish I had not asked /

BACH: Yes /

(He looks up from his desk.)

Yes / I wish you had not asked / it stains the memory of a man to know with his last breath he begged /

(ALWAYS leaves, broken. BACH ponders his disappearance. He descends from his stool. He leans against the desk. He exults, a silent writhing. A woman enters.)

2

BACH: You're bruised /

(The woman poses, defiantly.)

Beneath your eye / you're bruised /

(She stares at BACH. She moves languorously, stops, and regards him again.)

This bruise / which you have not attempted to disguise / is not the only bruise / is it? / the only bruise? / I might discover others / on your arms / and on your thighs / I have / I think / consciously or unconsciously / allowed myself to be complicit in your misdemeanours / or worse / yes / why deny it? / I have promoted them / actively promoted these mischievous encounters between you and others which / let us confess it / could properly be described as sordid / were it not for the fact that I / in my fascination with you / created a faith so frenzied that my pain became a ritual / necessary even / proof of the divine / kiss me / kiss me / and then it must stop /

(FELLTRAY frowns.)

Yes /

(Her mouth turns down.)

Yes / because /

(Her shoulders heave.)

NOTHING MUST DISTRACT ME FROM MY /

(She lets out an animal cry.)

DO NOT CRY PLEASE /

(She shakes her head. She bites her lip.)

NEITHER CRY / NOR SOB /

(She fights her inclination.)

I am a poet / and in the lives of poets / once only it appears / or twice at the most / a collision occurs / of mood and circumstance which /

(FELLTRAY is overwhelmed by grief. She turns away as a howl rises from her depths.)

SHUT UP / SHUT UP I SAID /

A collision which shakes the very foundations of his talent and /

OH / DO BE QUIET / FELLTRAY /

(She wails. He persists.)

Compels him to repudiate all those obligations of love and civility which / in normal times / he would gladly acknowledge as deserving precedence /

(He is adamant.)

THE POET MAY NOT VIOLATE HIS OATH / I SWORE AN OATH / I SWORE AN OATH TO POETRY /

(FELLTRAY rushes to BACH and wraps her arms about him. BACH declines to admit her intimacy. He lifts his hands in the air as she weeps on his shoulder. She recovers. She sniffs. She removes herself.)

FELLTRAY: How long will it take / this / this /

BACH: Poem /

FELLTRAY: Poem / yes / this poem? /

BACH: I don't know / it is a major work /

FELLTRAY: Yes /

BACH: With something so ambitious / so intransigent / so utterly draining of his resources / a poet would be rash to announce / even approximately / the time of its completion / the expense of energy / and of imagination / inevitably induces a frailty / a sickness / even a morbid exhilaration / which frequently obstructs the process /

(He observes the effect of his words on her.)

I think you would be advised to forget your intimacy with me and / however reluctantly / attach yourself to another man / the one / perhaps / who has so comprehensively beaten you /

(FELLTRAY stares at the floor. She collects her thoughts.)

FELLTRAY: You it was who /

BACH: Not now /

FELLTRAY: You who urged / no / more than urged / implored me to /

BACH: Not now / Felltray /

FELLTRAY: Go with unkind men / unkind / I use your phrase / and unkind is not the word / I'm telling you / for what they do /

BACH: *(Walking to his desk.)* I am writing the poem /

FELLTRAY: *(Without rancour.)* Go with unkind men / and bring home to you my gift of suffering / your phrase again /

(BACH sits on his high stool, clears his throat, and pretends to study his paper.)

I do these things / I don't know why I do / I go / I come back / I pose / bruised and provocative / exactly as you instruct me to /

(BACH coughs again.)

And you /

(She shakes her head, wounded, bewildered.)

And you /

(BACH is writing. His pen is audible in the silence.)

I think / to be humiliated for a man you love / for
some need he has / some pain which he manipulates /
converting its sordidity into a proof of your devotion / that
women can do / at least a woman can who loves as I love
you / even to the extent that when her face is smacked by
some lout in an unclean room / she hardly contemplates
the smack / but rather / how the smack might be
described / the pleasure the description will induce when
this / gift of suffering / I use your phrase / is spread before
him who is so adored humiliation vanishes /

(Pause.)

Bruising is not humiliation but standing here while you /

*(BACH suddenly slams his desk, screwing up the paper he has been
scrawling on and flinging it to the floor. The violence of his temper
ends FELLTRAY's meditation. She is quite still, then turns to go, as
if altered. She stops.)*

The old man in the yard / cleaning his tools / I said

BACH: Cleaning his tools? /

FELLTRAY: You look awful / lie in the shade / or go to bed /

BACH: Cleaning his tools? /

*(Pause. FELLTRAY is again, perfectly still. Suddenly she walks out
smartly. BACH slips off his stool. He throbs. He thrills.)*

She stood /

(He shakes his head in wonder.)

In the quicksands of her misery / in the swirling flood of
her spoiled life / she stood /

(He lifts his hands.)

Upright / arching her back / her arse high / and tight /
and the more gravely I injured her / the more keenly she
returned to the attack / oh /

(He shakes his head in fascination.)

And in the meantime / the old man / shamed by my
rebuke and on the point of death / thinks to retrieve his
honour by one last act of servitude / he cleans his tools /

(He laughs.)

And I said no need / no need for that /

(He laughter fails.)

And we will never meet again / not him / not her / not me /
never / oh / the tremendous fact of never /

(He wonders. He aches. A man walks in, brisk, grinning.)

Away Fuck / away Fuck /

(BACH abandons his meditation and skips up onto his stool.)

Away /

3

DETRIMENT: Great poetry /

BACH: Away Fuck / I beg you /

DETRIMENT: Is the sediment / left lying in the bottom of
a flask in which genius and banality have been mixed /
shaken / and boiled over a flame / you are genius / and I /

BACH: Fuck / please /

DETRIMENT: I am banality / and however intolerable I am
to you / I am necessary / even if I appear as yet another
obstacle to the completion of your task /

BACH: *(Fixing DETRIMENT with a stare.)* Away now /

DETRIMENT: So often / the eruption of the commonplace / a
workman hammering a floorboard / a postman knocking on
the door / whilst it appears detrimental to the exquisitely
contrived condition created by the poet for his meditations
/ acts as a stimulation / a discordant note which /
paradoxically enhances the harmony it had / at first sight /
threatened to destroy /

*(BACH tosses down a pencil with a clatter. DETRIMENT is charmed
by his own speculation.)*

Whilst we crave solitude and silence / this solitude and
silence must be enjoyed only as a pause / rather as a fish
leaps out the water / for one second / two perhaps / before
plunging back into the rushing river / longer and it would
suffocate / identically / if we made silence our permanent
state oh / imagine the obscure and unhealthy subjects upon
which we would concentrate our nerves / you need me /
Bach /

BACH: I am unhealthy / it is the condition to which I aspire /

DETRIMENT: You need me /

BACH: I don't need anyone / and my rare excursions into the airless corridors of intimacy serve only to remind me of the fact / every hour I have spent with others / even in acts of frantic nakedness / I regretted / so away / Fuck / because even now I am shuddering with a powerful resentment that will cause me to give you such offence you will leave here wishing you were dead / a trivial injury compared to the damage you inflict on poetry by intruding in a place where it must be obvious you are not now / and never were / wanted /

(They exchange a long, withering stare.)

Away / Fuck / be kind to yourself /

(BACH allows the stare to decay, then returns abruptly to his papers and seizing his pencil, scrawls. DETRIMENT watches. BACH seems to think, then writes, and thinks again, a parody of creativity.)

DETRIMENT: You are evil / Bach / evil as a child /

(BACH chews the end of his pencil, feigning thought.)

The way that children hurt / hurt things they love / torturing / then comforting / flinging a thing away / then howling to get it back again /

BACH: I shan't howl to get you back again /

(BACH writes, apparently. DETRIMENT shakes his head pitifully.)

DETRIMENT: And you're not writing anything / that page / obviously it's blank /

(Reluctantly, DETRIMENT goes to leave. He stops at the door.)

Felltray ran by / black-eyed / red-eyed / practically blind / she collided with me / why / Bach / why? /

(He shakes his head again, goes to leave.)

BACH: It isn't blank /

(He lifts the page.)

It says /

(He stops.)

You read what it says /

(He extends it, holding the page by its edge. DETRIMENT is wary.)

DETRIMENT: It is an insult to me /

BACH: Is it? / you'll never know unless you look /

(The paper remains in the air.)

DETRIMENT: I know you / Bach / you want me to resist you / and having resisted / to capitulate / and crossing the room / dog-like / slave-like / to suffer some humiliation which / whether or not it does me harm / delights and gratifies you /

(He grins falsely.)

I am happy to oblige /

(He marches towards BACH's desk. Immediately BACH screws the page into a ball and tosses it to the floor. DETRIMENT stops.)

BACH: You're right / it says you are pious / and a prig / and in retrospect I cannot imagine how I ever could have tolerated your proximity / were it not for the fact / the trivial and insignificant fact / that I was sleeping with your mother /

DETRIMENT: *(Patiently.)* Bach /

BACH: Fucking /

DETRIMENT: Bach /

BACH: Sodomizing /

DETRIMENT: *(Less patiently.)* Bach / I knew that /

BACH: And casually demolishing the mental and physical welfare of your mother /

(He glares at DETRIMENT.)

OF COURSE YOU KNEW IT / AND HOW HARD
IT IS TO INJURE ANYONE WHO TAKES SUCH
PLEASURE IN HIS INJURIES / AS YOU /

(Pause. BACH looks down at last to his desk.)

Fuck / listen to me / if our friendship had not been great I
never could have found such satisfaction in destroying it /
don't come back / will you? / and if you hear some rumour
of my misery / or my dying / still don't / still don't / it's all
I ask of you /

*(DETRIMENT goes out. BACH is motionless on his stool, his head
hanging. At last he climbs down. He walks thoughtfully, stops, plays
with his sleeves.)*

Love gone / love gone / and along with love / obligation /

(He plucks.)

The poet launders his soul /

(He smiles wanly.)

A soul which / because of its sensibility / requires frequent
laundering /

(He is entranced by his own metaphor.)

The poet's soul resembles a sheet / white and pristine /
which / no sooner is it spread over a bed / than the whole
world wants to lie on it / churn it into creases / and smear
it with ejaculata and excreta / THERE WERE TEARS IN
FUCK'S EYES / TEARS ROSE AND ROLLED / HE
COULD NOT DISCIPLINE THEM / and that's another
thing /

(He draws his shirt tighter in his ecstasy.)

In repudiating obligation / the poet is privileged to
witness / at such close quarters / hope dying / hope
fighting and then dying / as if a great mansion slid / floor

after floor / into a swamp that encroached on it / and
liquefied its very foundations /

(He exults.)

A POET REQUIRES SUCH THINGS / THE AGONY
OF OTHERS NOURISHES HIM /

*(He springs towards his desk and is mounting his high stool when
DETRIMENT lurches back into the room, a long, gurgling cry
emanating from him as he stabs himself repeatedly in the abdomen
with a domestic implement. BACH, horrified, clings to the stool as if
to a post in a storm, running his hands over his body in a wretched
parody of his friend's suffering. DETRIMENT's ordeal ends at BACH's
feet. BACH gazes down in the following silence.)*

In one sense / Fuck /

(BACH plays with his fingers.)

In one sense certainly / it could be argued / a gesture
of such / extravagant / proportions / places an onus
on me / to make of this poem something more perfect and
more powerful / then even I intended to / AND I DID / I
DID INTEND IT / BELIEVE ME /

(He chews his tongue.)

But I stated / only just now / I stated / out of your hearing
presumably / that I do not submit to obligation / NOT
EASY / FUCK / NOT EASY WHEN THE BLOOD IS
STILL GUSHING OUT OF YOU / BUT I WILL NOT
BE COERCED BY YOU /

*(He leaps off the stool and kneeling beside BACH's body, flattens his
hands in his blood.)*

YOU WILL / I PROMISE YOU / BE NEITHER IN /
NOR INFLUENCE / THE POEM /

(He raises his stained hands.)

You all / oh / all of you / you thrust your deaths at me /
you wield death like a club / you wave it like a banner /
it's only death / Fuck /

(A woman of 50 stands in the door.)

It's only /

(He is aware of her presence.)

It's only /

4

BACH: I said I sodomized you / I wonder if that did it? /

(He is casual.)

Some / like Fuck / are really / let's admit it / only waiting for an excuse to quit /

(He turns to face her.)

Take off your dress / and throw it on his body /

(She ignores him.)

One has to admit death / rather as a householder / however cautious / eventually admits a burglar by leaving open a door / or window /

(GLOVE drifts to the body and stands erect, gazing at the face.)

It must happen / it will happen / but need we dramatize it? / must we eulogize the burglar? / Fuck could have done this in the garden /

GLOVE: There is someone already in the garden /

BACH: Very well / there is a corpse already in the garden / in the stable / then / or in the cellar / but no / with his natural capacity for exaggeration he /

(GLOVE drags her dress over her head, and is naked. BACH watches fascinated as she lets the garment fall over the body of her son.)

And yet /

(He gnaws a finger.)

Am I not equally / if not more / entranced by the situation which you /

(His mouth is dry.)

Have added to /

(He aches.)

His /

(And yearns.)

Situation? /

(BACH stares fixedly at GLOVE, who gazes in stillness on the body of her son, a work of art not entirely contrived. BACH is suddenly vehement.)

How brilliantly you pose / and now I see it / it's blindingly obvious / Fuck died precisely in order to create the conditions for this pose / the two of you / for the first time / probably /and certainly the last / in perfect harmony / united for a purpose greater than either of you could possibly achieve alone /

(He thrills to his analysis.)

I have never / in my whole life / I don't hesitate to admit it / been so aroused / so tender / and yet / inflamed / by a woman as I am now by you /

(He sweeps on.)

AND NOT ONLY YOU / OH / NOT ONLY YOU / THE ENTIRE CONDITION IN WHICH YOU ARE ABLE TO BE SO MUCH MORE THAN YOU /

(He shakes his head with wonder.)

The moral / the immoral / the aesthetic / the barbaric / oh / everything / everything contributes to /

(He stops, a hand raised.)

Indeed death is wonderful / wonderful is death / but only from this point of view / it shines a strange light on the living / oh / how death illumines you / but you will not / separate or together / destroy my poem / the greatness of which / becomes more evident the more stratagems the world invents to obstruct its birth /

GET OUT OF MY HOUSE AND DRAG THIS
UNLOVED THING WITH YOU /

(He climbs back onto his high stool. Taking a single sheet of paper, he swiftly wipes his stained hands, screws the paper into a ball and tosses it down. He then assumes the meditative condition familiar to poets. GLOVE sustains her own pose. Time passes. Out of this silence, her breath, uneven and punctuated by sobs.)

It's a peculiarity of poetry / of all arts probably / that there comes a point at which / almost arbitrarily / further effort / whilst it might alter the outcome / simply cannot improve it /

(He sucks his pencil.)

Which is not to say the thing cannot be improved / that it is somehow perfect / not at all / but all the energy and ingenuity devoted to it merely serves to / what? / spin it round / spin it on its axis / whilst never actually moving it in any direction / rather as you see sometimes in a drain or gutter / a twig or leaf which / caught in opposing currents / simply whirls / whirls giddily /

(He smiles with a certain reluctance. He taps the paper with his pencil.)

This line is like that / five days I have been grappling with it / five days / and it is not perfect / I am so pained by the knowledge it is not perfect that I go to bed in such a state of anger I do not sleep / whilst all the time I sense / I know / it cannot be more perfect / that neither I nor any other poet could make it so / and what's more / the world beyond this room will never know its imperfection / it is / quite simply / intransigent / but to accept that it is intransigent / oh / that's another matter /

(He creates a small laugh.)

How satisfying it must be to have no notion of art / and to be / merely / a craftsman / to make a shoe or wallet /

to finish the shoe / to finish the wallet / without further
thought / look / you say / a wallet / ha /

(He shakes his head.)

No / I'm leaving it there /

(He drops the pencil onto the paper. He regards GLOVE with a certain anxiety.)

I have to have you / have you and possibly / yes / why
not? / sodomize you / in saying I had sodomized you I /
probably / we can never know / probably I drove Fuck to
his death / so /

(GLOVE merely returns his look.)

So it's / proper / proper even though / strictly speaking this
act did not precede / but followed on / my boasting it /

(He slips off his chair to go to GLOVE, who forestalls him by grabbing her garment, plucking it off the body of her son and covering herself. BACH stops in mid-movement.)

GLOVE: The poem /

(Pause. They exchange a slow stare.)

The poem and then /

(BACH looks at the floor.)

BACH: Yes / thank you I / thank you I so nearly infringed my
own injunction /

GLOVE: Nothing must be allowed to /

BACH: No /

GLOVE: Compromise / or /

BACH: Quite /

GLOVE: Influence /

BACH: Thank you again /

GLOVE: The poem /

BACH: I am grateful to you /

GLOVE: The poem is also sacrifice /

BACH: Yes /

(He nods vehemently.)

Yes / that is a very good word / sacrifice /

GLOVE: My sacrifice / and yours /

BACH: Both of us / yes /

GLOVE: Simply to gratify /and it would be simple / so simple for us to gratify our longing /

BACH: All right /

GLOVE: Whilst it would draw us deeper into our already so deep / so /

BACH: ALL RIGHT / I SAID /

(She concedes.)

The problem is / of course / now that I have allowed myself to / unleash / unleash this hound of longing /

GLOVE: Hound of longing /

BACH: Hound of longing / yes /

GLOVE: Good /

BACH: I now have the strenuous task of kennelling it again / a task which / frankly / might be more enervating and distracting than if I had simply /

GLOVE: No /

BACH: We had simply /

GLOVE: No /Bach /

BACH: Done the act / and forgotten it /

GLOVE: Bach / it could never be forgotten /

BACH: No / no / perhaps not /

GLOVE: Never forgotten /

BACH: No /

(GLOVE looks at him, a reprimand to his casualness.)

GLOVE: What is the poem / Bach? /

BACH: What is the poem? / what is the / what /

GLOVE: Yes / what is it? /

BACH: You would hardly expect me / I think to /

GLOVE: No /

BACH: Attempt to summarize the /

GLOVE: I mean / what is it for? / the poem? /

(BACH seems mortally hurt by the question, and shrinks away from her, feeling his way back to his desk and retreating not only to the high stool, but climbing onto the desk itself, dislodging papers as he fixes himself there, aloft and beyond interrogation. GLOVE now sobs from her depths, unaware of the arrival of four men in the doorway, discreetly attending.)

5

GLOVE hastens from the room. The undertakers, exquisite in decorum, advance towards the body of DETRIMENT. Briefly they gaze on the sight, then with practised moves, shake out black shrouds.

BACH: Bury me /

(The undertakers look up.)

Bury me / it's necessary / if not in my interest certainly in yours /

(They look at one another.)

You are about to raise a trifling objection / how should a man be buried if he is not dead? / but I ask you / I ask you who are specialists in the arcane science of decorum and disposal / why are the dead buried? / I suggest because / were the dead not buried / they would infect the living with plague and pestilence / precisely these considerations apply to me / my dreams / innocuous as they may be so long as they remain confined within the perimeter of my head / once mounted on poetry / ride out into the world with terrible effect / souls also sicken / believe me / souls choke / souls vomit / think of your wives / think of your families /

(They stare at BACH.)

AND I CAN'T STOP / I'VE TRIED / CUNT / SPORT / GARDENING / BUT NO / ONLY THE CLAY WILL STOP THIS TERRIBLE FLUENCY /

(He stares at them, wild-eyed. They shift uncomfortably. BACH shrugs.)

I go on /

(He looks from one to the other.)

I go on / if not with your encouragement / with your permission / God help you when / in years to come / you recollect this conversation / how someone you chose to think was mad implored you fill his mouth with earth / a single spadeful would have done / and how you denied him / tell your daughters / tell your sons /

(He descends from the desk.)

Not a conversation / I did all the talking / scarcely a conversation /

UMBER: *(Spreading the shroud.)* It's not a hole / the grave /

(The undertakers proceed to enclose the body.)

Many labour under this misapprehension / that graves are holes / put me in the grave / they say / I will do / I reply / but you must earn it / you must earn your grave /

(They take out cords.)

BACH: How should I earn it / then? / how should I earn my grave? /

(They seem preoccupied, passing the cords under the body.)

Presumably / by dying? /

(They work nimbly.)

You suffer / you die / and you are buried /

RIB: *(Drawing the cord tight.)* He thinks it's a hole /

BACH: I do / I do think it's a hole / if it is not a hole / what is it? /

(The undertakers regard BACH with more pain than resentment. BACH shifts uneasily under their collective gaze.)

Forgive me / you are understandably reluctant to allow an uninitiated stranger to diminish the dignity of your profession by reducing its complex rituals to the mere excavating and filling of holes / much / much more than this it is / I concede / and concede willingly / on the other hand / the grave remains a hole / even if / whilst being a hole / the hole is the least part of its significance /

(He regards them in turn. Their expressions are reproachful. BACH moistens his lips.)

RIB: *(At last.)* Write your poem / Mr Bach /

BACH: Thank you / I will write it /

RIB: Write it / and stop looking for excuses /

BACH: *(Piqued.)* Excuses? /

ALZARIN: Yes / do write the poem / Mr Bach /

BACH: I was not excusing myself when I invited you / in the interests of your children / and your children's children / to obstruct the creation of this poem / I was / in an unforgivable relapse into the worst kind of sentimentality / caused no doubt by the spectacle of the suicide of my only friend / putting the peace and prosperity of mankind above my own passionate and / some might say / obsessive / need to articulate the terrible and beautiful thoughts that are embedded in my poetry / no more of that / no / no more / no more of that / you encourage me to write the poem / I will write it / and God help all of you /

(He glares at the undertakers.)

UMBER: That's it /

BACH: That's what? /

UMBER: That's how a man earns his grave / Mr Bach /

(BACH's mind races. He looks from one to the other.)

BACH: And if / earning my grave / I draw a million others prematurely into theirs /

ALZARIN: *(Cutting him off.)* Their graves are theirs /

(BACH searches the faces of the undertakers.)

BACH: 'Their graves are theirs' /

(His mouth moves. He frowns.)

'Their graves are theirs' / yes / obviously / their graves are theirs / your lucidity is / even to me / who rarely flinches from a thought no matter how appalling /

(He shakes his head, as if bewildered.)

Your lucidity is /

(He shrugs.)

Chilling /

(The undertakers regard him coolly. BACH creates a laugh.)

It's /

(He bites his lip.)

Chilling /

(He laughs, again falsely.)

How I aspire / in every line I write / to be so chilling /

(The undertakers smile indulgently and stooping to the enshrouded body, hoist it and bear it away. BACH suddenly hurries to the door.)

I WRITE FOR YOU / I WRITE FOR YOU /

(He laughs, authentically now.)

YES/ YOU / THE PALL-BEARERS / THE GRAVE-DIGGERS / YOU / AND ONLY YOU /

(He drifts back into the room.)

Let no poet dare assume he speaks to every man / a preposterous ambition / he who speaks fastidiously speaks to the few / this few / this strong few / inflamed / impassioned / and intransigent / proceed to fling themselves on others / who / infected as if by some exquisite pestilence / do the same / seizing one another by the collar / in the market / in the bedroom / HEAR THIS / HEAR THIS YOU /

(He laughs at the thought. He shakes his head. He sniffs. He lifts his gaze to the high desk. He runs his tongue over his lips. He frowns. He falters. He sickens.)

Something about that desk /

(He shakes his head.)

Not that desk / any desk / implies discipline / implies duty / what is a poet / a clerk? / no / clerks have desks / not poets / desks inhibit creativity / they threaten / they coerce / AND THE STOOL'S NO BETTER /

(He frowns.)

The slow progress of this poem / if it is slow / and it is / of course / arguable that with the greatest works of art the rate of progress is no indication of their /

(He stops. He stares at the desk as if it threatened him.)

Value or /

(He stops again. He goes towards the stool. With a cruel thrust, he topples it. He studies the effect.)

Yes /

(He walks around the fallen stool.)

Yes /

(He frowns.)

So much obstructs the poem / the human obviously / but not only the human / the material / not only men but things / these things / whilst lacking consciousness or sensibility / nevertheless flock to the conspiracy / how often I have gone to write the single word / the one word both meaningful and musical / and pressing the pencil to the page / was rendered apoplectic by the sudden breaking of the lead / it is as if these inert objects participated in the administration of a law designed to frustrate brilliance and originality / so be it / are these not the permanent and possibly necessary conditions in which the struggle must be undertaken / yes / yes / they are / they are the conditions / and I accept them / I accept them as a duellist submits to the regulations that will govern the manner of his death /

(He kicks the fallen stool.)

Yes /

(And again.)

Yes /

(And again. He flinches.)

Ow /

(He nurses his ankle.)

I fight the stool /

(He kicks again.)

And the stool fights back /

(He laughs. Suddenly he is swept by a wave of loneliness. He walks, smoothing his hair with both hands, comforting his solitude. He stops. He looks out of his fear as if from a window. A child enters. BACH pulls a face.)

6

The child does not respond to this. BACH assumes his normal face. The two look at one another.

BACH: *(For want of anything better to say.)* The stool fell over /

(He senses her disdain.)

It did not fall over /

(He goes to the stool and rights it.)

I flung it to the ground /

(Made uncomfortable by her unfaltering regard, BACH rambles on.)

I was in a mood / a bad mood / I looked for something / or somebody / on which to vent my temper / and there was the stool / poor stool / it took the brunt /

(He runs a hand over the seat.)

All right though / all right the stool /

(He is provoked by her withering look.)

You should be grateful to the stool / supposing you had wandered deliberately or by accident in here / say ten minutes earlier / you might well have been the focus of my resentment / I should have pushed you over / I should have bruised your shins /

(He stares at the child. He nods his head with a certain gravity.)

I know what you are /

(The child is unmoved.)

You are the latest /

(BACH bites his lip, frowning, calculating.)

GET UNDRESSED /

(The child flinches. BACH laughs cruelly.)

You blinked / ha / you blinked / with one flick of mischief
I snapped the needle of your scrutiny / I don't like children
very much / even less do I like the obligation to be kind
to them / are children kind? / never in my experience /
gangsters / savages / torturers / nothing separates them
from their parents but degree /

(A pause, then the child bursts into tears, her shoulders rising and falling in her wretchedness. BACH climbs onto the stool and observes her. At last the tears subside. She lifts her eyes to BACH.)

Now / as you are aware / I am wholly and undividedly /
passionately and obsessively / wilfully and instinctively /
driven to write the greatest poem /

(The child jerks up her dress, revealing her underwear. Her gaze is fixed severely rather than seductively on BACH. BACH lowers his head. Pause.)

Of our time / when I ordered you undress / some little
time ago / the proposal was insincere / it was / far from an
authentic longing to see you naked / political in nature /
by political I mean /

(BACH is stopped by the child's refinement of her provocation. She walks up and down before him, the skirt of her dress hoisted in one hand. BACH turns away, with an affectation of patience, to avoid her gaze. But she is regimental, her pace, her gaze, unfaltering. BACH loses the contest in an explosion of temper.)

YOU WILL BE MURDERED /

(She marches on.)

YOU KNOW / YOU KNOW / YOU KNOW THE
MORTAL DANGER YOU ARE IN /

(She persists.)

AND I HAVE MURDERED / OH / MURDERED
AND MURDERED / A PITILESS MURDERER ME /

(Now she stops. She looks at BACH with pity. She lets fall her dress. BACH goes slowly to her. They kiss. They sink to the floor. Her knees rise. They are lovers, tender and discreet. The room slowly fills with the figures of ALWAYS, FELLTRAY, DETRIMENT, GLOVE, RIB, UMBER and ALZARIN, who form an audience, also tender, also discreet. BACH sits up. he seems thoughtful.)

I was kind /

(He looks at the figures clustered around.)

I was not angry / I did not murder / I was kind / and this kindness gave me pleasure /

(He searches their faces.)

I WAS EXCITED TO BE KIND /

(Some lift their shoulders in a gesture of incomprehension. They begin to drift out.)

YOU DON'T LIKE ME TO BE KIND /

(He staggers to his feet.)

YOU DON'T / DO YOU? /

(They shake their heads, regretfully. BACH turns to the child.)

THEY PREFER IT IF I MURDER YOU /

(He follows the departing figures to the door.)

I WON'T / I WON'T SATISFY THIS / THIS /

(He lacks the word. They go. BACH shrugs.)

This /

(He gives up the search. The child's wan expression causes him to smile. He puts a hand on her, tenderly.)

SADOVEE: I think you should /

(BACH is chilled.)

I think you should murder me /

(BACH frowns.)

IT'S WHAT I CAME FOR /

(She laughs brightly.)

I saw you in the newsagent / did you see me? / you
didn't / did you? / you did not see me / it was half-past
nine / the clock struck / the clock on the library / that
clock is fast /

BACH: Ten minutes fast /

SADOVEE: Ten minutes fast / so actually / it was not half-past
nine / but nine-twenty / does it matter /Bach / that I say
half-past nine? / it doesn't / does it? / I think history is
not facts / but longing / I saw you /Bach / and that was
history / Queen Katharine slept with a boy / in fifteen-
something / she was fifty-seven / so you see / it doesn't
matter / me being eleven / and you / I checked this /
forty-three /

BACH: Forty-one /

SADOVEE: *(Swiftly enraged.)* IT DOESN'T MATTER /BACH/
IT DOESN'T MATTER / IF YOU ARE FORTY-ONE
OR SEVENTY /

BACH: *(On the defensive.)* You said you checked / I only /

SADOVEE: IT DOESN'T MATTER / IT DOESN'T /
BACH /

BACH: No / it doesn't / possibly /

SADOVEE: BEAUTIFUL IS INACCURACY /

   (Pause. She swiftly laughs. Her eyes study his.)

   Say it / say inaccuracy /

   (Pause.)

BACH: Inaccuracy /

(Now she frowns.)

SADOVEE: You say it / but you don't like it / never mind /
we can't always agree / great longings / such as ours /
ours and Queen Katharine's / are not / surely / driven by
common interests? / hobbies / tastes/ reciprocities? /
no / it's longing / longing / longing / I can't shut up /
Bach / you will have to murder me /

(She is swiftly cross.)

IT'S NOT MY FAULT / YOU WERE IN THE
NEWSAGENTS WHEN I WAS / YOU DIDN'T HAVE
TO BE /

(She glares. She laughs.)

You're a composer / and I'm another interruption / I'm a
liability /

(She jerks her skirt away again.)

A LOVELY LIABILITY /

(She tempts with her eyes.)

Say I am / say I am a lovely liability /

(He is thrilled, but resists her.)

BACH: Not a composer / but /

SADOVEE: IT DOESN'T MATTER / BACH /

BACH: No /

SADOVEE: WE HAVE AGREED /

(Now they both laugh, but he is wary.)

BACH: Still / a composer must compose / mustn't he? /
even if / strictly speaking / he is not a composer? /

(He goes to move to his desk. SADOVEE is severe, rigid, intransigent.)

SADOVEE: Bach /

(He stops, her voice deeply authoritative.)

This quarrel between us / if it is not resolved / will lie / like some deep fault / in the foundations of our marriage / it will heave / and strain / and we shall hear the groan of it / however high the tower we choose to spend our nights in / side by side we'll stare into the dark / cold and hating / stop it / stop it happening /Bach /

(BACH is paralyzed, as if by dread.)

BACH: *(At last.)* Marriage? /

(He manages to turn to SADOVEE.)

SADOVEE: Darling / why do you think I came? / why do you think you kissed me? / for mischief? / for mischief only? / no man as great as you / seducing a child / makes love for mischief / I knew / and so did you / when our eyes met / this was / oh / darling / we both knew / please / I so dread the slightest sign of poverty in you /

(BACH is trapped. His hands make futile moves.)

Still your hands /

(He looks at his hands.)

Still your hands /Bach / those pointless gestures detract from your dignity / my darling /

BACH: Yes / yes / they are /

(He shrugs.)

They are /

SADOVEE: Silly /

BACH: Silly / yes /

SADOVEE: As if / unable to speak / you let your hands describe your reluctance / you are not reluctant / darling / are you? /

BACH: Reluctant? / no / not me /

SADOVEE: I so dread the slightest sign of weakness / hesitation / or cowardice / in you / my darling and wonderful composer / you are not weak / if you feel weakness / say so / come to me / and I will offer you my breast /

(She looks down at herself.)

Small now / my breasts / but soon / soon /Bach /

(Her face is a picture of hope. BACH is moved, his reason abolished.)

BACH: I said I killed / killed others / strictly speaking / that is not true / I let them die / with you however / half my heart says murder her / hence this difficulty I have in breathing / because the other half says no / she is beautiful / and I should give my entire life to you / the heart's a single organ and cannot have two rhythms / if I am to live / then I must choose / I do / I do choose / I choose you /

SADOVEE: *(At her most womanly yet.)* Darling / darling /

BACH: *(Exhilarated.)* Feel my heart / feel it /

(He kneels before her. She inserts her hand into his shirt.)

SADOVEE: Beating /

BACH: Beating / yes / and all its quarters in harmony /

(They exchange looks of profound relief.)

SADOVEE: Compose now /

(She is radiant.)

Compose a symphony so / oh so /

(She touches his face. She senses the slightest pain in him. She frowns.)

BACH: *(A decision to abolish the facts.)* I will /

(He creates a smile.)

I will /

(He stands. He goes towards the desk.)

SADOVEE: *(Standing and brushing her dress with a hand.)* Or make love if you want to /

BACH: No /

SADOVEE: No / the symphony /

BACH: The symphony first /

(Inspired, he ascends the stool. He takes a pencil. He chews the end. He shifts. He squirms. SADOVEE observes him with a maternal indulgence, half-pride, half-anxiety. BACH, lifting his eyes from the page, meets her regard. They smile awkwardly. BACH returns to his labour. He chews. He shifts. SADOVEE walks up and down, dreamily, patient, bored as a wife. She drifts to a stop, gazing over the country.)

SADOVEE: I'm going to the newsagent's /

(Pause.)

The newsagent's / Bach / did you hear me? /

(Pause.)

The newsagent's /

BACH: Good /

SADOVEE: The newsagent's /

BACH: Good /

SADOVEE: The newsagent's / I'm going to the newsagent's /

BACH: Good /

SADOVEE: The newsagent's / The newsagent's /Bach /

BACH: Good / good /

SADOVEE: It is good / isn't it? /

BACH: It is good / certainly / good that you /

SADOVEE: GO TO THE NEWSAGENT'S /

(A terrible stare holds them. BACH bites his lip. With a spasm of energy he swings about on his stool and writes. The pencil lead snaps off. He flings the pencil down and seizes another. He is engrossed, absent. SADOVEE examines the hem of her school dress.)

It's torn / this / above the knee / if I go out like this God help me /

(She is rigid with dread.)

Ditch / field / old shed / spindly trees / discarded plastic / mattress / drain / etcetera / drain /

BACH: Shh /

SADOVEE: DRAIN /

BACH: *(Ferocious.)* SHUT UP / SHUT UP / SADOVEE /

(She seems satisfied by BACH's swift rage.)

SADOVEE: I like that / I like the way you say my name / say die / say die / Sadovee /

(Pause. BACH is writing fluently.)

BACH: Of course I will not / silly / say die /

(And writes, not lifting his head.)

Silly /

(And writes.)

Silly /

(SADOVEE looks again at her torn dress. She deliberately extends the tear. Still BACH does not look up, in spite of the characteristic sound of ripped cotton. SADOVEE goes a little way, looks back, but BACH is lost in his creation.)

SADOVEE: Her little life / her little life / as if she paid the world a visit / and seeing it / said on consideration / it does not suit me / and the big lives / the big lives / and the long lives / seeing them /

(She shakes her head.)

SEEING THE BIG LIVES /

(She shakes it vehemently, with disgust.)

I love you / Bach /

BACH: *(Scratching the paper in his fluency.)* I love you /

(She waits for more. He gives nothing more. She goes out. Only now does BACH lift his head and cease. He hears a resounding emptiness. He contracts from within. From this shrunkeness, an uncanny laugh, not cruel. He surges.)

PAGE /

(He plucks the page and flourishes it.)

PAGE /

(He vaults to the floor.)

And this page / this single page / whilst being only the first of five / or seven hundred pages / were it by accident / mischief / or catastrophe / to be discovered on its own / blown by a firestorm from some blazing library / washed through sewers and sun-dried on a lonely marsh / limp but legible / the one would say / the one who retrieved it / I thank my God this fragment is all that now remains / I thank my God because reading it my soul somersaulted / not only my soul / also my brain / how terrible therefore / if I had read the whole / my life would have been exploded /

(BACH smiles curiously.)

An imperfect logic / no one who read this page could find his old complacency again /

(He ponders.)

PAGE TWO /

(He goes to clamber on the stool. He is obstructed by a thought. He retreats. He stares at the desk. The stare endures. He decides. He lifts the lid. Something falls out. It is a child's shoe. He looks at it, without stooping. He looks again at the desk. He draws out SADOVEE's torn and besmirched dress. He frowns. He lets it fall to the floor. He reaches in again. He draws out her frail pants. He wonders. He is unaware he is observed.)

7

SEPTEMBER: And is that Heaven / Mr Bach? / how is that Heaven? / I so want to know /

(She stares, her hands in her deep coat pockets. BACH looks up. He is thoughtful, unabashed.)

The dull us / to me that is a cotton fragment / with a shred of elastic threaded through / the dull us / but what is it to you? /

(She advances a pace or so. She gazes at BACH, who studies the pants a little longer, then decisively consigns them to the desk. He jumps down from the stool.)

BACH: I am a landowner /

SEPTEMBER: We know that / Mr Bach /

BACH: And my father / who in many respects was more artistic than me / and certainly more civil / planted whole groves of trees /

SEPTEMBER: A beautiful estate /

BACH: A beautiful estate my father bequeathed me / whereas I have done little to improve it /

SEPTEMBER: A pity /

BACH: Arguably / but without decay you would not applaud the tantalizing fragility of his creation / and / since you invoked Heaven / we can safely say of Heaven / if you walked in it / you would never call it Heavenly /

SEPTEMBER: Wouldn't I / Mr Bach? /

BACH: No / its routine charm / its absolute perfection / would make you yearn for chaos / slums / fire and aridity /

SEPTEMBER: Would I? / Mr Bach /

BACH: You know you would /

SEPTEMBER: The dull us / I think I see enough of slums /

BACH: PRECISELY /

(He waves a hand vaguely in the air.)

Your familiarity with slums and killers causes you to like both my estate / and me /

SEPTEMBER: I don't like you / Mr Bach /

BACH: Everyone likes me / And those who / for reasons which are hard to grasp / withhold this liking / nevertheless recognize my necessity / I am not a killer / but killers even / serve /

SEPTEMBER: Serve to what? /

BACH: Excite the landscape /

SEPTEMBER: I do not understand a word of your /

BACH: You do understand /

SEPTEMBER: The dull us /

BACH: You understand me perfectly /

SEPTEMBER: Dull we are / but where would you be without us? / I ask that frequently /

(She swerves.)

I LOVE THE DULL / THE SAD AND LOVING DULL / ON WHOM YOU FIX YOUR JAWS / EXOTIC YOU / SUPERFLUOUS WE / FIELDS OF US / KIND AND COMMON / you are a child-killer / the whole world hates you / but you luxuriate in that / no doubt / the rage / the notoriety / everything you said constitutes a confession /

BACH: Possibly / and it is perhaps / not only redundant / but also / oddly unaesthetic / to say I did not do it /

SEPTEMBER: Yes /

BACH: Yes / the fact that I did not do it should not be allowed to stand in the way of the exquisite resolution that insists I did /

SEPTEMBER: Yes / these artistic considerations are compelling /

BACH: *(Laughing.)* They are / they are / you see / you do understand me / you are not dull / the police are poets / how could you not be / all night in doorways / your wet capes shining in the street lamps / your burning torches flash / the livid masks of whores and /

(He stops. He looks at SEPTEMBER.)

SEPTEMBER: You are not seducing me / and your poetry belongs to another age /

(SEPTEMBER's rebuke causes BACH to flinch. He frowns. He stares resolutely at the floor.)

Now / surrender little Sadovee's clothing / please / poor little Sadovee /

(BACH seems lost.)

Her clothing / her clothing / Mr Bach /

(He is distracted, but obeys, opening the desk and removing the relics.)

Her never-husband / her never-holidays / her never-family /

(SEPTEMBER shakes her head.)

BACH: *(Troubled.)* How do you mean / another age? /

(He offers the items. SEPTEMBER, removing a plastic bag from her pocket, holds it open. BACH stuffs in the garments.)

Do policemen no longer stand in doorways? /

SEPTEMBER: Not if we can help it / Mr Bach /

BACH: Or encounter whores? /

SEPTEMBER: *(Tying the neck of the bag.)* Inevitably / but not by torchlight /

BACH: DON'T WALK AWAY / THIS IS A SERIOUS MATTER /

(She stops, puzzled.)

A VERY SERIOUS MATTER / TO SAY OF A POET THAT HIS POETRY LACKS CONTEMPORANEITY /

SEPTEMBER: Did I say that? /

BACH: YOU SAID THAT / YOU SAID THAT /

SEPTEMBER: Contempor– /

BACH: YOU SAID THAT /

SEPTEMBER: I cannot say the word /

BACH: NEVERTHELESS / YOU SAID IT /

(SEPTEMBER watches him suspiciously, coolly.)

SEPTEMBER: I have reason to believe that you have killed a child / your outdated metaphors /

BACH: You see? /

SEPTEMBER: Are of no interest / either to the law / or me /

BACH: OUTDATED METAPHORS / YOU SEE? /

(SEPTEMBER regards BACH, disdainfully.)

The form of the poem / the means by which the poem comes to its audience / and enters in / and damages / and leaves its imprint as a marauding army /

SEPTEMBER: Marauding army? / we do not have marauding armies / Mr Bach / where have you been? /

(BACH is further wounded. His face is strained by a deep dread. His eyes search SEPTEMBER's face.)

BACH: You are telling me / you are /

(He gnaws.)

You are describing my /

(He swallows.)

Irrelevance /

SEPTEMBER: I hope you serve a hundred years / Mr Bach /

(He looks at her, without resentment.)

And if there were galleys / I would have you chained
to an oar / and more than that / I'd have the sea
forever turbulent / so you were both sick / and flogged
/ simultaneously / poor little Sadovee / your father /
planting his trees / might have expected them to civilize
his son / but no /

BACH: No /

SEPTEMBER: It was not to be /

BACH: Trees / we exaggerate their tenderness / they also kill /
by stealing light / horrible is the forest / and no police / to
stop the great elm throttling the sapling ash /

(He extends his single page.)

SEPTEMBER: Is that what you did? /

BACH: Read this /

SEPTEMBER: Throttle her / throttle the little sapling Sadovee? /

BACH: Read it /

SEPTEMBER: Everything you utter / confirms your guilt /

*(She looks at him without rage. BACH's hand remains outstretched.
The poem hangs in the air. At last SEPTEMBER advances and takes it.
She looks at BACH a long time before letting her eyes fall to the page.
She reads. He watches her reading. At last her eyes lift again.)*

I'll burn these / you can't be trusted /

(She thrusts the page back at BACH. She is swift and efficient.)

Her fragments / half-consumed / you'd seize them out the flames / kiss them / hurt your mouth / no / we have an incinerator / tremendous centigrades /

(She walks smartly to the door.)

I'll shut the door / shall I? / or do you like it open? / the view / the scented air / beautiful / or are they distractions? /

(Her hand is poised at the door.)

Shut it / shall I? / or leave it open? / you say / you say /

(BACH merely looks.)

I would like you to say / so like you to say? /

(She bites her lip.)

SHUT THAT DOOR /

(She laughs strangely.)

Or /

(She trembles.)

LEAVE THAT DOOR OPEN /

(She dares not meet his eyes. Failing to elicit a reply, she marches off, clutching the plastic bag. BACH listens to her receding footsteps. He is pensive. On an impulse he flings to the door and calls.)

NOT DULL / NOT DULL / THE UNDULL YOU /

(His shoulders fall. He darkens. He seems paralyzed.)

So it is true / the man Bach writes great poetry /

(He frowns.)

AND SHE WAS SENDING YOU TO THE GALLEYS / FLOGGING / TEMPESTS / A GREAT GALE OF OUTRAGE STORMING THROUGH HER SOUL /

(He reflects.)

Then she read him / Bach / she read Bach and she knew / he had to live / dead children notwithstanding / AND SHE'S POLICE / SHE KNEW ONE DEAD CHILD NEVER IS ENOUGH / a single page did this / page one / immortal is page one / immortal and terrible / page two / page two /

(He goes to move, but his limbs resist him. He falls heavily. He cries out in pain. He lies still. At last he speaks from his ordeal.)

His own body thwarted him / as if flesh knew the damage Bach might do flesh / and policed him /

(He yells.)

WELL YES / THE POLICE ARE BOTH OUTSIDE AND INSIDE YOU /

(He smacks his thigh. A figure watches. As ever, BACH senses him.)

8

BACH: He's paralyzed /

(The figure walks in, curious. He stares down at BACH's inert body.)

Paralyzed is Bach / I warned him / always warning him / you can't do everything you want to do / ruling the world and so on / fetch a pillow / but he's stubborn / can you take dictation? / any pillow / just go through / bedroom on the right / he has this way with words / that's very nice / I say / but you should soothe / not irritate / soothe / life's cruel enough without you / soothe for God's sake /

(The figure gazes down placidly.)

Are you a foreigner? / pillow / it's a /

(He stops.)

Thing to suffocate the unloved with /

(Pause.)

Or possibly the loved / the loved whom we think too tender for the harsh and / do you take dictation? / remorseless character of existence / page two must be dictated /

(Pause.)

You are apprehensive / you have a premonition / that if page one can strip a policewoman / not of her garments / a thing perhaps not difficult to do / but of the law / what more awful acts queue one behind the other / fratricide / patricide / matricide / etcetera / which the genius of Bach will unlock / as if a madman flung open the cages of a zoo? / do fetch a pillow / the way he fell /Bach / he aches /

(BACH's weary gaze strains to meet the stranger's eyes. The figure seems to consider BACH's invitation. He goes out. As BACH lies fixed to the floor, a face appears round the door, peering. The return of

the stranger, bearing a pillow, causes the face to abruptly withdraw. The stranger looks at BACH, holding the pillow to his chest, as if undecided.)

MCNOY: I don't know / I don't know what to do /

BACH: I told you / place it under his neck /

MCNOY: You told me / yes / but that's you / I said <u>I</u> did not know what to do / I / I / not you /

(BACH affects patience. The stranger ponders.)

BACH: The stanzas / similes and so on / piling up / an ocean is page two / do fetch a pencil /

(MCNOY ignores BACH's plea.)

And he will dictate /

(A contest develops.)

Bach will dictate / you / never mind the spelling / you will commit the words to paper /

(Pause.)

Gratitude will flow in profusion / I own four thousand hectares / wooded / pastured / vined / fetch a pencil / Mr

MCNOY: McNoy /

BACH: Mr McNoy /

(BACH loses patience.)

OR WRITE IN BLOOD / WHAT IS THE MATTER WITH YOU? / DO YOU HATE BEAUTY? /

(Instantly.)

Now I've forgotten the first line / no / I haven't / yes I have / I have /

(He screws up his face in his ordeal.)

The whole world will condemn you / Mr McNoy / your
name will be a curse / a verb will be made from you / to
watch while perfect inspiration perished on the
floor / lethargy and bovine indifference / it will be said
of lovely things so miserably destroyed / THEY WERE
MCNOYED /

*(BACH cannot resist a bitter laugh. The effect on MCNOY is
electrifying. He flings aside the pillow and surging towards BACH,
proceeds to rain kicks on him. BACH shakes like a doll. The face
reappears at the door, now a mask of horror and screaming.)*

SADOVEE TWO: DAD / OH DAD /

*(BACH cries out as his body is driven across the floor by MCNOY's
violence.)*

OH DAD / DAD / PLEASE /

*(MCNOY ceases, more from exhaustion than remorse. He gazes on
the wreck of BACH.)*

MCNOY: His I / his me / his fucking I / his fucking me / the
me – ing cunt / the I – ing cunt / ANY I NOW? / ANY
ME? /

(BACH is still.)

Sorry / darling /

SADOVEE TWO: Oh / Dad / oh / Dad /

MCNOY: Sorry / sorry /

(He turns away from his deed.)

Pillow over there / sorry / darling /

(He suddenly erupts again.)

TAKE DICTATION /

(He takes a final swinging kick at BACH.)

TAKE DICTATION HE TELLS ME /

SADOVEE TWO: DAD /

MCNOY: Sorry / sorry / darling /

(MCNOY shakes his head, moving away from the scene. SADOVEE TWO advances squeamishly to the motionless BACH. She lets out a weak cry.)

PILLOW / PILLOW /

(He gestures vaguely towards the pillow. SADOVEE TWO retrieves it and returns to BACH. She looks down, her face ghastly.)

And then he says /

(MCNOY shakes his head in disbelief.)

HE SAYS TO ME / TO ME /

(He turns his head to SADOVEE TWO.)

Do I hate beauty? /

(SADOVEE TWO ignores her father.)

HE SAYS THAT TO ME /

(He boils again.)

I SHOULD HAVE SAID / WAS SHE NOT BEAUTIFUL? / MY LITTLE GIRL? / MY SADOVEE? /

SADOVEE TWO: *(With resolution.)* I'll finish him off /

MCNOY: That's what I should have said /

SADOVEE TWO: I'm finishing him off /

MCNOY: Finish him off / then /

(He composes a sentence.)

I think of clever answers / but only afterwards / only retrospectively /

(SADOVEE TWO kneels beside BACH.)

If these clever answers came quicker / I might not resort to violence /

(SADOVEE TWO presses the pillow over BACH's face, leaning with her whole weight.)

It's having the vocabulary / the vocabulary could well abolish the necessity for violence / in my case / though not in every case / he had vocabulary /

(SADOVEE TWO lifts the pillow to study the effect of her exertions.)

A considerable vocabulary /

SADOVEE TWO: Still breathing /

MCNOY: Did it stop him hurting your sister? / quite the contrary /

SADOVEE TWO: I'll try again /

MCNOY: He employed it / I imagine / to define the nature of his depravity /

SADOVEE TWO: *(Pressing down again.)* Poor man / poor man /

MCNOY: He had these urges / devils possibly / and giving them a name made them familiar / possibly / familiar and therefore /

SADOVEE TWO: *(Weeping as she leans.)* Poor man /

MCNOY: Legitimate /

(He swiftly boils.)

ARE YOU CRITICIZING ME? /

(SADOVEE TWO abandons her efforts, tears away the pillow and flings it across the room.)

SADOVEE TWO? / ARE YOU? / ARE YOU? /

(She shakes her head. MCNOY sinks. He shrugs pitifully.)

Criticize / oh / criticize if you want to /

(In a spasm of pity, SADOVEE TWO goes to her father, who repudiates her. They stand forlornly.)

See what we can do for him /

(MCNOY goes to the mess of BACH. He frowns. He kneels. He nurses his own neck contemplatively.)

I don't know if /

(He is incompetent.)

I don't know what /

(He discovers a handkerchief and applies it ineptly to BACH's wounds. SADOVEE TWO drifts to the pillow and sits on it, drawing up her knees and hugging them.)

SADOVEE TWO: She was a sacrifice / Sadovee One /

(MCNOY purses his lips.)

What's that I said / it's when you have to die / she said / I'm a sacrifice / and so are you /

(MCNOY stares grimly.)

MCNOY: Why did you come here / Sadovee Two? /

(She frowns. She shrugs. Suddenly she bursts into tears, the last of her infancy. MCNOY watches. At last she is silent. MCNOY's gaze returns to BACH.)

I injured Mr Bach / injured him horribly / but how horribly he injured me /

(He casts a pained look at SADOVEE TWO.)

He had to suffer / and because he suffered / I can be /

(He shrugs.)

I feel /

(He grapples with himself.)

I almost feel /

(With a relief.)

POOR BUGGER / WE HAVE SUFFERED EQUALLY /

SADOVEE TWO: *(Contemplating the beauty of MCNOY.)* The bond of hurts /

MCNOY: What? /

SADOVEE TWO: The bond of hurts /

MCNOY: *(Puzzled by SADOVEE TWO's observation.)* Probably /

(SADOVEE TWO jumps up with determination.)

SADOVEE TWO: Wash him /

MCNOY: *(Stimulated by her.)* Wash him / yes /

SADOVEE TWO: Flannel / towels / etcetera /

MCNOY: *(Gesturing offstage.)* Third door / on the right /

SADOVEE TWO: *(Gazing and earnest.)* What a big house /

MCNOY: It is / it is a big house /

SADOVEE TWO: But we require it /

MCNOY: Do we? /

SADOVEE TWO: *(As she sets off to the bathroom.)* Oh yes /

(She turns.)

THE DIMENSIONS OF THE HOUSE WILL DICTATE THE DIMENSIONS OF THE POETRY /

MCNOY: Poetry? /

SADOVEE TWO: He is a poet / Mr Bach /

MCNOY: Yes / he is / he is a poet / a poet obviously /

(They look at one another. SADOVEE TWO skips away. MCNOY cries out.)

THE POET CAN'T SPEAK / I KICKED SPEECH
OUT OF HIM / THE POET IS FOREVER SILENT /
SADOVEE /

(He writhes. He shakes his head. He lifts his hands, and lets them fall again. SADOVEE TWO reappears in an apron bearing a basin and sponge. She is resolute and calm.)

SADOVEE TWO: Speech is one thing / but speech is not synonymous /

MCNOY: *(Bemused by his child's eloquence.)* Synonymous? /

SADOVEE TWO: Not synonymous with poetry /

(MCNOY stares.)

Is it? /

(She advances on the still form of BACH.)

I put lunch on / I initiated /

MCNOY: *(Again puzzled.)* Initiated? /

SADOVEE TWO: The whole process of domesticity which is so necessary if we are to create the conditions under which imagination might be lent the fullest and unfettered /

MCNOY: Unfettered? /

SADOVEE TWO: *(Kneeling by BACH.)* Opportunity for expression / it is one thing to imagine but quite another to express /

(She peers at BACH.)

His eyes are open / but you're perfectly correct /

MCNOY: Am I? /

SADOVEE TWO: He will never speak again /

(She turns a bold, uncritical face to her father.)

Never /

(MCNOY's gaze falters. He looks to the floor.)

And that places on us an onus which /

MCNOY: *(Frowning.)* Onus? /

SADOVEE TWO: *(Irritably.)* ONUS / ONUS YES / ONUS
MEANING /

(She stops. She gazes at her father. She fathoms swiftly.)

I placed /

(She half-laughs.)

I chose to place the word /

(She jumps to her feet.)

Onus /

(She offers the sponge to MCNOY.)

Adjacent to the words /

(MCNOY accepts the sponge, gazing at SADOVEE TWO.)

On us /

(She marvels.)

AN ONUS ON US / you heard it / you heard me /

MCNOY: What does it mean / onus / Sadovee? /

SADOVEE TWO: *(Crossly.)* IT DOESN'T MATTER WHAT IT
MEANS / it's the music of the words / father /

MCNOY: Father? /

SADOVEE TWO: I have taken it from Mr Bach /

MCNOY: Taken what? /

SADOVEE TWO: Poetry /

MCNOY: You make it sound like a disease /

SADOVEE TWO: Yes / probably it is / and I have caught it / I have caught poetry /

(MCNOY looks down at BACH. Swiftly he delivers a savage kick which causes the body to lurch. SADOVEE TWO screams.)

FATHER /

MCNOY: *(Repudiating her.)* FA – THER / FA – THER / WHAT'S THIS FA – THER / I'M NO ONE'S FATHER / I'M DAD OR NOTHING / I'M YOUR DAD / SADOVEE /

(He sends another kick towards BACH.)

SADOVEE TWO: All right /

MCNOY: HE HAD ONE GIRL / HE CAN'T HAVE THE OTHER /

SADOVEE TWO: All right /

MCNOY: *(Running at BACH again.)* NO ONE TAKES TWO GIRLS OFF ME /

SADOVEE TWO: *(At her most passionate.)* DAD /

(SADOVEE TWO's submission stops MCNOY in mid-kick. He falters. His leg declines. He is thoughtful. SADOVEE TWO goes to him, and places her head on his shoulder.)

It's all right to have poetry /

(MCNOY seems unconvinced. He shrugs.)

The dilemma /

MCNOY: Dilemma /

SADOVEE TWO: The dilemma is / whose poetry is it? / does it come from him / or does it come from me? / what are the origins /

MCNOY: *(Resigned.)* Origins /

SADOVEE TWO: Of this abundance of metaphor and simile /

MCNOY: *(Moving gently away.)* Simile /

SADOVEE TWO: Am I merely his /

MCNOY: Toast burning /

    (He takes refuge in mundane tasks.)

SADOVEE TWO: His /

    (She shrugs.)

MCNOY: Toast / darling /

    (He goes out. SADOVEE TWO looks at the inert BACH.)

SADOVEE TWO: His /

    His /

    His /

    (She shrinks.)

    Oh / Sadovee One / was it better to be you / then me? /

    (She undoes the strings of her apron, and removing it, goes to the desk as if to drudgery. She climbs on the high stool as BACH, like the lid of a sarcophagus, is raised and tilted, half-convalescent, half-deity.)

9

The scratching of SADOVEE TWO's pen on paper. A handful of admirers clusters at the door. Pages drift down as SADOVEE TWO responds to her inspiration. At intervals, she stops, puzzles, strains. Then, driven on, she writes furiously. Now MCNOY appears, aproned and transporting a tray of glasses, which he diligently proffers to the visitors. They advance further into the room. They observe both the writer and the source. BACH's eyes move, all the rest is paralysis. One or two of THE CURIOUS, bolder than the rest, advance further into the room and twisting their heads, attempt to read the fallen pages.

OBLAST: Seventy /

    (He pulls a face.)

    Seventy /

    (The accompanying visitor looks to another.)

BOLLY: Seventy /

    (Another sheet of paper drifts down from the high desk.)

HAYDN: Seventy /

    (The visitors digest the information as SADOVEE TWO works on. One of them observes the still form of BACH, swirling his drink in the glass. He wants to speak. He does not know how. His eyes rise and fall to BACH's. The tension is broken by SADOVEE TWO, who slams down her pencil.)

SADOVEE TWO: *(Crossly.)* Stuck /

    (She shakes her head.)

    Stuck /

    (She jumps down from the stool and marches out of the room. MCNOY immediately enters.)

MCNOY: Glasses / glasses please /

(The visitors, intimidated by MCNOY's brisk manner, place their glasses on his tray. SADOVEE TWO enters at once, exercizing her fingers as if about to recommence. The visitor standing before BACH does not move as MCNOY advances on him with the tray. MCNOY is patient. The visitor recalcitrant.)

STAYS: I think of the great poets / Always I think of them / I think why are they great? /

(He stares at BACH. MCNOY's fingers fidget ever so slightly.)

I was at a university / not any university / the greatest of all universities / where wise men taught me / and wise women / some black-haired and ambitious / some tired and grey / and cramped in their rooms we argued / aching to understand not what the poets wrote / but why the things they wrote were beautiful / the rooks cawed in the meadows / the shadows lengthened with the dying of the day / and still we argued / still we strained / and always it came back to this single word / humanity /

(MCNOY seems to stiffen. He looks at the floor. Suddenly he drops the tray. The glasses smash. The tray rolls. MCNOY is perfectly still.)

A single word / four syllables / such a big word you might think it required more / eight / ten syllables / no / it carries its significance in four /

(MCNOY grinds a glass under his heel. STAYS is unimpressed.)

I am myself a poet /

(Now MCNOY sends the tray flying with a vicious kick. It wails and stops.)

How good it is / my poetry / I could not say / less good than Mr Bach's / less good in every way / but one /

(STAYS looks down.)

The one being / sadly for Mr Bach / the one that / as we discovered during those afternoons of rooks and shadows / constitutes the greatness of great poets /

(He creates a smile.)

I think rather than repeat the word / I should be on my way /

(STAYS goes to set off.)

SADOVEE TWO: *(Cruelly.)* MIND THE DOGS /

(STAYS stops.)

They bite / for no apparent reason / packs of them / and nearly wild /

(STAYS is casual.)

STAYS: Mr Bach requires protection / obviously /

SADOVEE TWO: *(Going to her high desk.)* Homer kept a dog / Virgil had three /

STAYS: Pets / Miss / pets /

(MCNOY breaks his own tension by kicking the tray from the room, aimless as a bored child. BACH's eyes travel from one to another.)

The servant /

(He invents a different smile now.)

I have observed this frequently /

(The tray flies.)

As if to compliment his master /

(And flies again.)

Interprets his attitude / his values /

(MCNOY boots the tray against the wall.)

even his morality /

(MCNOY is rigid with suppressed rage.)

In a vulgar and somewhat exaggerated form /

(He suffers. His fists are clenched.)

Indicative / nevertheless / and an indictment surely / in this instance / of a loveless / turbid / and /

(STAY's prosecution is cut off when MCNOY collapses, flapping and dying.)

SADOVEE TWO: FATHER / OH / FATHER /

(SADOVEE TWO flings from the high stool and rushes to the twitching and expiring form of MCNOY.)

OH / FATHER / MY DEAR / MY DEAR / DEAR FATHER /

(SADOVEE TWO cradles the head of MCNOY, her hands moving over his face and body compulsively. As she sobs in her loss, STAYS observes, infatuated. Like a photographer, he shifts and squirms from place to place, enjoying one perspective after another. MCNOY is still.)

Dad I mean / I mean Dad /

(MCNOY is gone. SADOVEE TWO touches his face lovingly.)

Don't be violent / I said / don't be violent / Dad /

(She shakes her head.)

HE SHOULD HAVE BEEN / HE SHOULD HAVE SMACKED YOUR /

STAYS: DON'T MOVE /

(She is surprised, and obeys.)

Don't move / oh / how beautiful you are / in grief / how beautiful like that /

(STAYS studies SADOVEE TWO, like a connoisseur. SADOVEE TWO turns her head to him.)

Never in this room / ever / beauty like that /

(SADOVEE TWO's gaze turns towards BACH. STAYS is smitten.)

DON'T YOU SEE / THE BEAUTY OF THAT? /

SADOVEE TWO: *(Inspired.)* Writing /

(She goes to move.)

STAYS: DON'T GET UP /

SADOVEE TWO: Writing /

STAYS: I TOLD YOU / DON'T GET UP /

(He makes a swift move to SADOVEE TWO and smacks her face. She reels. She stares.)

Kiss me /

(She frowns. STAYS' face becomes a mask of rage. He takes her face between his hands and plants a passionate kiss on her lips. He separates himself from her.)

GRIEVE /

(SADOVEE TWO is contemptuous.)

KISS /

(STAYS launches himself at SADOVEE TWO and kisses her again, identically. She is cold. Her stare is rigid.)

GRIEVE / GRIEVE /

(She does nothing.)

GRIEVE / I SAID /

(She is recalcitrant.)

NOW KISS /

(He goes to her again. She turns away her head.)

KISS / KISS I SAID /

(STAYS smacks SADOVEE TWO. He glares in desperation. She yields nothing. Suddenly STAYS breaks out in a fit of weeping. He staggers away. He confronts the form of BACH.)

I BLAME YOU / I BLAME YOU FOR THIS /

(He lifts a hand to strike BACH. The hand falters. BACH's eyes are closed.)

Probably /

(STAYS is calm. His hand falls to his side.)

Probably /

(He smiles thinly.)

And probability is not desirability / probably Bach must exist / as wars must / and cruel regimes / these brief intoxications / the bands play / the slogans spread faster than disease / men do vile things / men not themselves vile necessarily / it's like a dream from which they wake / saying / did I do that? / was that me? /

(Two strangers peer round the door. STAYS notices them.)

IT WON'T LAST /

(They look puzzled.)

Your fascination with /

(He gestures towards BACH.)

Can't last / can't stand up to scrutiny / the rooks / the shadows lengthening /

(The strangers gawp.)

The lengthening shadows / and the rooks / we discriminate you see / as evening falls / the rooks returning to the trees / wise men and women / a little tired / unsurprisingly /

(STAYS drifts out. UMBER and ALZARIN advance into the room, discreet as ever. The third and fourth undertakers follow them in.)

10

The sound of ferocious barking in the distance. The undertakers, infinitely tactful, wait for SADOVEE TWO to detach herself from MCNOY's body. They then lift it and bear it away. SADOVEE TWO drifts after them, lingering in the doorway. BACH's eyes open.

SADOVEE TWO: *(Intuiting this.)* Coming /

(She sniffs. She shakes her head in her loss.)

Coming / I said /

(She cannot tear herself away from the door. She takes deep breaths. At last she turns and strides to the desk, erect and efficient.)

Seventy-one /

(She writes swiftly, but simultaneously weeps. The pen and the weeping are a complimentary music. The sheet falls to the floor.)

Seventy-two /

(She inscribes. Her tears ebb away. Only the pen is audible.)

Seventy-three /

(The sheet falls. SADOVEE TWO starts another. The rate of her inscription declines. It drags to a stop. Her pen is held aloft. At last her head turns to BACH. She quotes the previous half-line to him.)

'Sky flotsam and baked bone you' /

(He is still, as ever. SADOVEE TWO is patient.)

'Sky flotsam and baked bone you' /

(SADOVEE TWO runs a finger round her lips. She taps the pen against her teeth.)

'You' what? /

(The pen taps.)

'Sky flotsam and baked bone you' /

(Nothing emerges from BACH. The pen falls silent. SADOVEE TWO lays down the pen with a characteristic sound. She slides off the high stool. She walks a little, thoughtfully.)

You see /

(She frowns.)

You see / Bach / we /

(She struggles to express her thought.)

My sister / and my dad and me / the clan McNoy / the McNoy family / scum of the earth / all three of us / but dignified / dignified / Bach / by one thing / sacrifice /

(She looks directly into his eyes.)

We sacrificed ourselves to poetry /

(BACH stares into SADOVEE TWO. She turns away.)

So /

(She wrings her hands.)

GIVE IT / BACH / GIVE THE POETRY /

(He can only stare. SADOVEE TWO senses the arrival of another party of THE CURIOUS at the door. She waves them away with a violent gesture.)

NOT TODAY /

(Her vehemence causes them to back away like cattle.)

You want to be yourself / Bach / propped against the wall / thinking your own thoughts / fed and watered regularly / you may not / Bach / you may not think your own thoughts / you're mine / you're theirs / you're property /

(THE CURIOUS edge in, fascinated. SADOVEE TWO launches herself at them.)

NOT TODAY / I SAID /

(They recoil once more. She looks longingly at BACH.)

Bach / you are / as I am / no more than the means by which our age articulates itself / its essence / its morals / its economy / you are a mouth / Bach / be a mouth or else /

(She screws up her face.)

I'LL POKE YOU WITH SOMETHING / SOMETHING SHARP AND SPITEFUL / I'LL DO IT / BACH / I'M A MCNOY / THERE'S MUCH OF MY DAD IN ME /

(The bravest of THE CURIOUS, compelled by desperation, peers round the door and calls for the satisfaction of his hunger.)

TABLET: Seventy-three /

(He grins feebly. He is emboldened.)

Seventy-three /

(SADOVEE TWO prods BACH with a finger, at first tentative, then with more conviction. BACH's eyes widen with shock. THE CURIOUS set up a chant, half-laughing but growing in cruelty.)

THE CURIOUS: SEVENTY-THREE / SEVENTY-THREE / WE WANT SEVENTY-THREE /

(Stimulated by the raucous atmosphere, SADOVEE TWO now grabs the pen from the high desk and advances on BACH. She looks into his widened eyes. She stabs. She trembles. She stabs again. THE CURIOUS inch into the room, chanting. SADOVEE TWO becomes compulsive and simultaneously, imaginative in her cruelty, looking for vulnerable places to puncture BACH's skin. THE CURIOUS, observing the fallen pages, annexe them, quarrelsome as children. TABLET, to satisfy both his own craving and that of THE CURIOUS, reads out loud from the seized sheet, his eyes squinting as he interprets the handwriting of SADOVEE TWO.)

TABLET: SEVENTY-THREE /

(He reads loudly and disjointedly.)

'Furplaneyouflamethisgemrootcastingrootmiranda prosmirandaprostitute'

(Another snatches the page from TABLET.)

GNATCH: 'Somewarwastrickedtobursthebowelofdimboys' /

(Another snatches the page from GNATCH.)

GIVE US THAT / GIVE US /

(They tumble. THE CURIOUS fall upon the second loose page.)

TABLET: SEVENTY-FOUR / SEVENTY-FOUR /

(As they scrap, SADOVEE TWO persistently tortures BACH. Two pages being read out loud simultaneously, there is no sense made of any of it. Tears fill BACH's eyes, of pain and revulsion. SADOVEE TWO is suddenly exultant.)

SADOVEE TWO: HE GOES ON / HE GOES ON /

(She goes to race to the high stool. She is obstructed by the raucous and disorderly readers of the poem. To her dismay she sees one page is plucked from two sides.)

YOU WILL TEAR THAT PAGE / YOU WILL TEAR THAT PAGE /

(The page is ripped down the middle as she speaks. In the appalled silence, SADOVEE TWO is imperial.)

The page is destined for the printer / you may not tear the page /

(THE CURIOUS are sheepish and hang their heads.)

Give me the page / the two halves of the page / and clear the room / walk quietly to the station and take the train / when you reach the city go directly to the bookseller / place your order for the second volume / and having placed your order wait / wait patiently as five million others wait / the waiting is important and an element of the greatness of the poem / naturally you will ache with anticipation / ache / and rage / you will ring / and write /

and endlessly complain / and worse / as with all books / there will be delays / this also is necessary /

(THE CURIOUS extend the damaged pages to SADOVEE TWO. She receives them graciously. She goes smartly to the high desk.)

AND MIND THE DOGS /

(She ascends and is instantly engaged.)

'Sky flotsam and baked bone you' /

(THE CURIOUS drift away, abashed. One remains, unobserved by SADOVEE TWO, who writes feverishly as before. This individual approaches BACH and gazes on him. Again, the silence is emphasized by the scratching pen.)

BULOW: He's bleeding /

(SADOVEE TWO neither hears nor heeds.)

He's bleeding /

SADOVEE TWO: *(Indifferently.)* Is he /

(She hastens on.)

SEVENTY-FIVE /

(The sheet slides off the desk. She starts another. BULOW surreptitiously produces a handkerchief. He moistens a corner with his lips, and assuring himself that SADOVEE TWO is not watching, he attends to the cuts, kindly if inexpertly. He stops, the handkerchief in mid-air. He pulls a face.)

BULOW: He's /

(He shrugs.)

He's pissed /

(If SADOVEE TWO hears, she is indifferent.)

Excuse me / he's /

(SADOVEE TWO stops writing, but not as a consequence of BULOW's remark. She stares ahead, thoughtful, pained.)

He's pissed himself /

(She slowly turns her face to BULOW.)

SADOVEE TWO: It's not important /

BULOW: Isn't it? /

(Her gaze disconcerts BULOW.)

No /

(He shrugs unconvincingly.)

It's only piss /

(BULOW is suddenly indignant.)

ISN'T IT IMPORTANT? / I THINK IT IS /

(He looks from BACH to SADOVEE TWO and back again.)

SADOVEE TWO: Why do you think this man exists? / this scratched / and paralyzed / and urine-saturated man / ask yourself why he exists /

(BULOW shrugs.)

ASK YOURSELF /

(BULOW is not given time to reply.)

To sprawl in cafes with a fixed grin? / to push children on swings / to sit in manicured gardens as the sun sets / champagne in one hand / and with the other fondling the unhitched tits of some stolen wife? / what do you think Bach is? / a sentimentalist? /

(BULOW is abashed.)

Wash him if you want to / but we are under no obligation to be kind to him / and he knows this /

(SADOVEE TWO slips off the high stool.)

The brain of the poet is akin to a glass left out in a garden
overnight / the climate of his time drains into it like dew /
we admire / we adore / but should we not be more adoring
of those who suffered to inspire it? / whose sacrifice was
wrung out / hung out / dried and shredded by the sun /
think of the war poets without war dead / think of Bach
without Sadovee One /

(BULOW frowns.)

These last pages are poor / for the first time in his life Bach
wrote poor pages /

*(She snatches the last uncompleted page from the desk and screws it
into a ball. At the same time she rips the fallen page with her heel.
BULOW stares in mute horror.)*

It's perfectly possibly if / as you suggest / we neither
washed nor fed him / the extreme discomfort / and the
hallucinations induced by starvation / might cause him
to produce another page / though I suspect the style of
this last page would be incompatible with the rest / and
damage his reputation / no / it's best he /

(She stops, feeling the critical gaze of BULOW.)

And I'm /

(She looks at BULOW darkly.)

I'm /

I'm /

I'm /

(She pouts.)

Thirty / and want to go dancing / hip to hip with some /

(She shakes her head.)

HIP TO HIP /

(BULOW frowns.)

WITH SOME / AND IN THE TANGO / IN THE
MIDDLE OF IT / IF I HEARD BACH / IF I FELT
BACH COMING THROUGH ME / I'D DO MORE
JERK / I'D DO MORE TWIST / AND CRUSH MY
PARTNER'S HAND / I CAN RESIST / I CAN RESIST /

*(She glares defiantly at the puzzled BULOW, who bites his lip in
his agony.)*

BULOW: But you're / you're the /

(He seems about to weep.)

THE SOLE INTERPRETER /

SADOVEE TWO: I am / I was / I am / I /

(She tilts up her chin.)

Yes /

(She sniffs.)

Yes /

(She smiles falsely.)

But the work's done / I have redeemed the debt incurred
by my father / and I'm entitled to some /

BULOW: *(Howling.)* YOU ARE THE SOLE
INTERPRETER /

*(SADOVEE TWO repudiates BULOW with a look and marches from
the room. BULOW's fists open and close in his pain. SADOVEE TWO
passes back through the room with a suitcase and goes out of the door.
After a few seconds, the barking of the dogs. The barking ceases.
BULOW observes the pages attacked by SADOVEE TWO, lying on the
floor. He goes to them. He turns the torn shreds around to fit. He
begins to read. He is exhilarated. He hurries to the door and calls
after SADOVEE TWO.)*

IN WHAT WAY POOR? /

(She is distant.)

POOR IN WHAT WAY? /

(He writhes with indignation.)

THAT IS A SUBJECTIVE JUDGEMENT BASED
ON A SINGLE READING / A JUDGEMENT WITH
WHICH I / FOR ONE / CANNOT AGREE /

*(No reply comes. BULOW, crestfallen, returns with the damaged
pages between his fingers.)*

On the contrary / on the contrary / what Bach reveals in
these extraordinary and admittedly untypical pages is a
capacity for / lightness / joy / one might describe it as a /

(He shrugs. He pouts.)

Paradoxical frivolity /

(He is pleased with his definition.)

Yes / yes / as if laughter in a threatened garden was /

(He stops.)

'Threatened garden?' /

(He darkens.)

'Threatened garden' /

*(Half-reluctantly, BULOW is drawn towards the high stool. He goes
to climb up to his servitude. He senses his loss. He weeps, deep moans
come from him as he mounts to his seat. He picks up SADOVEE
TWO's pen. It scratches on the empty page. Deep moans surge from
him as he writes…)*

*

SLOWLY

'The Process of Disappearing…'

Strabo, '*Geography*'

Characters

SIGN	A Woman of Profound Conformity
CALF	" " "
BELL	" " "
PAPER	" " "

Four women chalkwhite in abundant silk, black. They are imperial in gesture, which is to say, spare.

|

SIGN: We can be burned /

    (All are silent.)

We can be burned / shall I make the case for burning? /

    (They incline their heads.)

The case for burning turns on what occurs when women are not burned /

    (They are pensive.)

I will describe the fate of dead but unburned women / and after you may say / you may / despite this harrowing account of /

    (Her mouth hardens.)

How they /

    (She perseveres.)

What they /

    (She alters the position of one hand.)

Still say we prefer to be unburned / you may / and this preference will be respected /

    (All four are exquisitely still.)

The civilized die many deaths /

    (She alters the position of the same hand.)

They tear away your skirts / and looking on your bare arse / your never-ever-lit-by-sunlight arse / jeer /

(She allows the image to penetrate.)

And having jeered / they spit / many of them / many / they queue to spit /

(And again.)

Some spit from hatred / others to make you wet / they want you wet / between your legs they want you wet /

(Her hand makes the identical move.)

So letting fall their sordid garments they can enter you / and jerking your knees in filthy fists / parody the intimacy none of us knew but some guessed / smacking and biting / chewing the whole ear off your head and rubbing raw your ribs till the red bones pierce the white kites of your chests /

(Her mouth is dry.)

Whereas burned / whereas burned /

(She is vehement, ecstatic in her repudiation.)

STRIP ASH / CAN THEY? / STRIP ASH NAKED? /

(SIGN surpasses herself.)

ASH-FUCK / CAN THEY? / FUCK ASH? /

(She is defiant, then ashamed. Her head falls. The other three gaze ahead. They appear to contemplate. At last one speaks.)

CALF: Conversely /

(SIGN's head rises again.)

Conversely /

(CALF is measured.)

We four dead and strong / placed / not flung / clean / disdainful / will make their hands fall to their sides / their tongues go dry with shame / behold these women / they would not tread the earth we trespassed on /

behold them / behold / such strong death / they will be engulfed by their own poverty / I say behold / behold the body / the same cannot be said of ash / behold the ash / it is / I think / ungrammatical /

(There is no visible response to CALF's proposition for some time.)

SIGN: *(Contrite.)* I was thinking of myself / I was thinking /

(She frowns.)

Of my own body / of this body which /

(She frowns more deeply.)

Has / for my lifetime / constituted what I call myself / but which is /

(Her head falls.)

Only an aspect of myself /

(She gazes fiercely at the floor.)

CALF: *(Helpfully.)* The greater part of self /

SIGN: Yes /

CALF: Whilst inhabiting the body /

SIGN: Yes /

CALF: And describing it /

SIGN: Yes /

CALF: Is not the body /

SIGN: No /

CALF: There is body / but how the body walks /

SIGN: Is not the body / no / I was coming to that /

(CALF is rebuked and silent. SIGN summons her powers of concentration.)

How the body walks is / who we are / how we have been /
how we have thought / in saying my own body /
therefore / I /

(She struggles with the thought.)

Simultaneously / deceived myself / but also / denigrated
my parents / my people / and /

(She lifts her head abruptly.)

Ha /

(She indicts herself.)

'I was thinking of myself' / did I say that? /

CALF: You said that / yes /

SIGN: 'My self' / did I really? / yes / I did /

CALF: You did /

SIGN: I did / I did say 'my self' / the unprecedented intensity
of the crisis we find ourselves in explains this possibly /

CALF: I am certain of it /

SIGN: Words / concepts / whose stability and permanence we
have assumed / suddenly /

BELL: Like walls /

SIGN: Suddenly /

BELL: Like stones /

SIGN: Topple /

*(BELL's intervention creates a stasis. The women maintain their
rigidity. BELL's mouth reveals her anxiety at uttering the thought
which follows.)*

BELL: In debating how / the manner in which / our bodies
might be deposited for the scrutiny / and desecration /
of our enemies / whether they should be whole or ash /

we have / consciously / or unconsciously / assented to a premise /

(She hardly dares articulate the subject of her enquiry.)

The premise that /

(She struggles.)

The premise /

SIGN: *(With a slight gesture.)* Shh /

(BELL is silenced. The women are constrained, breathing in unison. At last BELL's eyes close in a spasm of pain.)

BELL: I have to state the premise /

(No one responds. BELL is encouraged by this.)

I am stating the premise /

(She is about to expound when SIGN intervenes.)

SIGN: IF /

(BELL is silenced by the syllable.)

IF /

(BELL opens her eyes, staring at the floor.)

If you state this premise / you will be stating it for one reason / and only one / to invite us to inspect it /

(SIGN is calculated in her delivery.)

In inspecting it / the possibility arises that it might be argued / and dissented from / it cannot be dissented from /

(BELL is menaced but dares proceed.)

BELL: Very well / it cannot be dissented from /

(She summons up her resources.)

It cannot be dissented from / so great is its authority / but may it not be stated? /

SIGN: *(Contemptuous but patient.)* State it /

BELL: In stating it / what violence can be done to its /

SIGN: *(Cruelly.)* STATE IT / YOU ARE A HYPOCRITE / BUT STATE IT /

(BELL lifts her gaze.)

BELL: The premise is / we must be dead /

(Having gained this point, BELL does not know how to proceed. The women are silent. SIGN does not condescend to comment. BELL is again emboldened.)

But is this /

CALF: Thank you for stating the premise /

(CALF's intervention is decisive in destroying BELL's initiative. For a while the women are silent and immobile. Then one cries out.)

PAPER: FETCH HIM /

(The rest experience this shock as leaves shake on a tree, then are still. PAPER proceeds to relieve her tension in a tirade which affects to be frivolous.)

I must say / I must say I find this funny / very funny / if funny is the word / yes / funny is the word / I find it funny that the soldiers who / the soldiers we / the soldiers with their badges and their feathers / our own soldiers who swagger down the middle of the street / having failed miserably to cut the throats of the soldiers of the enemy / as if to compensate them / as if to reward them for their cowardice / and possibly their treachery / end up cutting ours / I call that funny / you may disagree / we must be dead / of course / very / very dead / and soldiers / they're experts / obviously /

(She bawls.)

FETCH HIM /

(She is immediately whimsical.)

Funny / so funny /

(They return to silence.)

CALF: I entered my mother's garden /

PAPER: *(As if stung.)* FETCH HIM /

CALF: *(Undeterred.)* My mother's garden / which is long / a garden of the long variety / two hundred fruits grow there / two hundred / in alleys / and at the end of every alley is a chair / she said /

(She stops her narrative. Her hands, folded on her lap, exchange places.)

Discover me /

(She stops.)

The gardeners watched me / smiling and sweeping / they did not dare indicate her whereabouts / nor did I ask / so rarely are we permitted to enter our gardens I did not care if it occupied the entire day / the branches are trained not only for fruit / but also shade / three times I passed her / so perfect was her stillness /

(As if in awe of her own experience, CALF very slightly lifts her chin.)

Our ancestors made the garden / and what they had made / she herself became / she was water / she was stone /

(They absorb CALF's metaphor. She is suddenly lightened by recollection.)

So she called my name / and I was / oh / I was /

(She permits herself the smallest and mildest laugh.)

Nearly standing on her toes /

(The smile fades. She is pained.)

When you say dead / I hear how terribly the word hurts you / as if existence were a law no one could disobey / but we may pass judgement on existence / to impose further existence upon ourselves for no reason other than that we exist already /

(She concludes the argument with a small, dismissive movement of one hand, a gesture of contempt.)

Of course / the knife hurts / but not worse than a wasp that gets inside your clothes /

(They are intimidated by CALF's authority. Their heads decline. Again it is BELL who risks a proposition.)

BELL: They may not trample it /

(CALF stares ahead. BELL discovers the will to proceed.)

They may not smash the fountains / or drop dead animals down the wells / they may /

(BELL expects to be interrupted. When she is not, she continues.)

As they beheld our bodies / clean and properly arranged / beholding the garden /

(Now she weighs the words.)

SIMPLY GAZE /

(BELL anticipates a withering riposte which does not come.)

SIGN: *(As if meditative.)* The barbarian gaze /

(She seems to prepare a reply to BELL'S suggestion, but is overtaken.)

PAPER: FETCH MY WASP /

(SIGN is patient. When certain that PAPER has completed her interjection, she proceeds.)

SIGN: The barbarian gaze / the beholding / the gazing /
the peculiar paralysis which subsumes the instinct of
barbarians / a soporific loss of will / a decay of temper /
they genuflect / they wander dazed from garden to
temple / from kitchen to pavilion / neither stealing fruit
nor killing birds / and letting fall their weapons / stand
amazed before our /

PAPER: WASP NOW / TIME FOR THE WASP /

SIGN: OUR TERRIBLE SOPHISTICATION /

(All are perfectly still. SIGN proceeds.)

Who ever saw this? / Who ever witnessed it? / You invoke
this gaze / the gaze of the barbarian / but are you invoking
it / or inventing it? / it pleases you to endow the barbarian
with civility / a poor and rudimentary civility / I wonder
why / could it be / perhaps / that if he possessed the
slightest capacity for culture / he might be civilized / and
you need not die? /

(SIGN holds her anger behind her teeth.)

And now it is legitimized / your cowardice / I have let a
sordid argument enter the room / as if some vermin /

BELL: She said gaze / not me /

SIGN: Crept beneath the door /

BELL: She said gaze / and I repeated it /

SIGN: Its filth-encrusted fur /

BELL: I repeated it to comfort her /

SIGN: Moist and odorous /

BELL: REPEATED IT / I SAID /

SIGN: Can you smell it? / can you smell the fur? /

*(BELL seems to shrink. SIGN's mouth is tight with fury. The silence
is dense.)*

CALF: We are talking across one another /

SIGN: *(Contrite.)* Yes /

CALF: Never did we /

SIGN: Never / no /

CALF: Talk across each other /

SIGN: No / I am doing it now /

(Her head shakes shortly and violently.)

I am so disturbed / I am so / so terribly disturbed /

(Her head declines. She struggles with herself. None of the others comforts her.)

They will not gaze /

(She persists.)

They will pause / pausing is not gazing / in this pause / the immense gathering of disgust /

(She lifts her head, restored.)

Forgivable perhaps / this habit we have / of assuming strangers envy us /

(She nearly smiles.)

The civilized die many deaths /

PAPER: *(Venturing.)* Now the rat's got in the room / was it a rat? / now the rat's in /

(Their silence emboldens her.)

Its smelly fur / etcetera / notwithstanding /

(She is afraid but longing.)

I /

(She abandons the attempt.)

Not saying /

(Her head declines.)

CALF: Good /

PAPER: Is it? /

CALF: Good / yes / good you are not saying /

BELL: Imagine them fucking you /

(It is as if this utterance were not heard. But only she can fill the hiatus.)

I do /

SIGN: *(Gravely.)* The rat is /

BELL: Often /

SIGN: The rat is certainly in the room /

BELL: Often I imagine it /

SIGN: *(Her tone dominates.)* We will undo our costumes at the throat / when we have exposed our throats we will call him /

BELL: This fucking causes me to vomit /

SIGN: He will be uncomfortable / never having seen our throats / but we will reassure him / let him go left to right so I / unless you see reason to deny me this precedence /

BELL: Because I vomit /

SIGN: Am first / first to have the knife / put to my throat /

BELL: They fuck me again /

SIGN: PUT TO MY THROAT /

BELL: Why? /

SIGN: PUT TO MY THROAT / I / EVEN I / AT THE POINT OF DEATH / STILL I /

BELL: I'm smothered / smothered in this vomit /

SIGN: *(Shaking her head.)* PREFER THE EUPHEMISM /

BELL: AND THEY FIND IT BEAUTIFUL / VOMIT THEY FIND BEAUTIFUL / WHY? /

(An intensely-sustained silence. At last SIGN fills the hiatus with a gesture of one hand.)

SIGN: I am loosening my collar /

(Her fingers work.)

Please /

(Her fingers stop.)

Don't make me do this on my own /

(Their faces are stiff with pain. SIGN is paralyzed.)

You dislike me /

(They are rigid.)

Strongly dislike me /

CALF: No /

SIGN: And the depths of this dislike /

CALF: I do not dislike you /

SIGN: Is a pretext / a pretext for not following my example / she is so commanding / I know what you say / so manipulative / coercive / where she goes she thinks everyone should go /

CALF: None of us says this /

SIGN: No? / then copy me /

(The challenge goes unanswered. SIGN masters her frustration.)

Oh /

BELL: The situation is /

SIGN: Oh /

BELL: Very /

SIGN: Oh /

BELL: Very /

SIGN: Do you hear my oh? / I fill this oh / never did a woman make such meaning from her oh / it is the oh of the dead / the dead are in it / oh / my loved ones / oh /

(They do not dispute SIGN's authority.)

'The situation is very' /

(She is patient.)

Let that be your epitaph / let it be inscribed above the door of your /

(She discovers the word.)

Kennel /

(Suddenly.)

No / not kennel / that dishonours dogs / aren't dogs loyal? / apologies to dogs / what dogs are / you are not / hutch /

(She is satisfied with this refinement.)

HUTCH /

(SIGN is calmer by virtue of expending her contempt.)

Call the guard now / call him / and say one throat only to be cut / one throat out of four / in that equation he will register the decay of our whole culture / he will understand the war was lost long before the war / but be careful /

(She is supreme in her disdain.)

Having cut my throat kindly / his dismay might turn to anger / and rather clumsily / he could slash yours /

(They are intimidated.)

Hurry / or the barbarians will be through the gates and the poor man will never get away / we do not ask our servants to die / do we? / whereas they expected it of us / not comprehending / in their ignorance / how /

(She is at her cruellest.)

What did you say? /

(She permits herself a savage smile.)

HOW VERY THE SITUATION IS /

(Her triumph feels complete to her. PAPER is oddly stimulated.)

PAPER: It won't work /

(She is combative.)

One corpse / lying in the sun / one / burned or unburned / they'll hardly notice you / it's all or none /

(PAPER's intervention is unsupported. SIGN is patient, sensing their capitulation. CALF's intervention is immaculately timed.)

CALF: None /

(The word is a wound to SIGN, whose hand, still poised at her collar, declines with infinite slowness to rest in her lap. A peculiar laugh escapes BELL'S mouth.)

SIGN: Shut up /

(BELL cannot.)

Shut up /

(BELL tries to contain the laugh by deep breathing.)

You disgust me /

(BELL inhales.)

Do you hear? /

(BELL heaves.)

You disgust me /

(BELL snorts, sniffs, recovers.)

Snot is pouring from your nose /

(BELL sniffs.)

This snot / this pouring torrent of snot /

(BELL swiftly draws the back of her hand across her face.)

With which you have now smothered your clothes /

(BELL'S shame is complete.)

This snot is your worth /

(BELL weeps.)

How thickly it flows /

(BELL gives herself up to despair. Her dishevelment is a contrast to her first appearance.)

CALF: You are humiliating her /

SIGN: Yes /

CALF: She loves her life /

SIGN: IT IS NOT HER LIFE SHE LOVES / IT IS LIVING / AS FOR YOU /

(She fills the word with her deepest contempt.)

BEHOLD /

(For the first time of all the women, SIGN turns her head to study CALF's profile, a cruel rupture of etiquette.)

BEHOLD /

(CALF is not injured. BELL snorts. This snorting threatens to subvert SIGN'S withering gaze. SIGN delivers a handkerchief from her own sleeve and extends it to BELL. BELL receives the gift. She dabs her nose, afraid to make a sound. She then offers it back to SIGN .)

Keep it /

(BELL is grateful and withdraws her hand, clutching the handkerchief.)

Why I am so scrupulous about handkerchiefs I don't know / when I never cry /

(Slowly, CALF turns her head to meet SIGN'S steady and contemptuous gaze, again infringing the rule.)

CALF: Cry now /

(The invitation and its implied rebuke causes an almost tangible resentment in SIGN, expressed through her unfaltering gaze. The tension destroys PAPER's frail equanimity. Rising to her feet she runs all round the women in an unconscious parody of a death throe before resuming her place. The shock of this causes BELL to shudder with apprehension.)

Cry /

(SIGN frowns, disturbed by the delicacy of CALF's proposition.)

SIGN: You want to weaken me / you want to see me weak before we die /

(Her bewilderment is authentic.)

Why? /

(CALF tries to fathom this for herself, but unable to articulate it, she emits an uncanny cry, her gaze fixed on SIGN all the while. This serves to unleash PAPER , who again is launched, runs, and resumes her place. Now CALF turns her head violently to the front.)

CALF: We are disappearing /

SIGN: *(Without temper.)* Yes /

CALF: Disappearing /

SIGN: Yes /

PAPER: In one form / disappearing in one form / reappearing in another / I know three words in their language / three's adequate / with three a woman can get by /

(PAPER exudes hope.)

TELL YOU THE WORDS / SHALL I? /

SIGN: *(Coolly.)* Do not dare /

BELL: Yes /

SIGN: *(Countering BELL.)* Do not dare /

BELL: Please /

SIGN: Equip this woman for servitude /

PAPER: BABY / WANT / I /

BELL: Baby? /

PAPER: BABY / WANT / I /

(BELL registers the sounds. PAPER laughs, half-hysterically.)

CALF: We are disappearing /

BELL: *(Rehearsing.)* BABY? /

PAPER: *(Helpfully.)* WANT / I /

BELL: And this / this means? /

(Now it is SIGN who abruptly rises to her feet. For a moment, PAPER and BELL are intimidated. Then PAPER proceeds, shamelessly.)

PAPER: These words / few in number /

SIGN: Slave /

PAPER: Diminish anger / and at the same time imply we relinquish any /

SIGN: Utter /

PAPER: Pretension to superiority /

SIGN: Utter /

PAPER: Furthermore /

BELL: *(Struggling with foreign words.)* BABY / WANT / I /

SIGN: SLAVE /

PAPER: Furthermore / possibly without them realising it / the speaking of these words implies a contract /

BELL: *(Memorizing.)* Baby /

PAPER: A contract which / even between enemies / is /

BELL: Want I /

(She looks to PAPER.)

Want / I? /

PAPER: Immortal and infallible /

BELL: *(Swiftly and certainly.)* BABY WANT I /

PAPER: THE CHILD /

(Her complacency is studied.)

It won't look like / it won't be like / or even sound like / those babies we called ours / but /

(PAPER turns to SIGN.)

The civilized die many deaths /

(The prospect of further life suddenly fills PAPER with a volcanic energy.)

I CAN'T KEEP STILL / I CAN'T KEEP STILL /

BELL: BABY / WANT / I /

(PAPER stands again.)

PAPER: This stillness / this stillness / why / why / why did we keep still all the time? /

(She sits and immediately stands again.)

CALF: *(With a forced equanimity.)* Because /

PAPER: I don't want to be still /

(She jumps up.)

CALF: Because /

PAPER: IT'S BAD FOR THE LEGS / IT'S BAD FOR THE ARMS /

(PAPER laughs shrilly, and stops the laugh.)

CALF: Because we cannot discipline the world if first we have not disciplined ourselves /

BELL: *(With a determination.)* BABY / WANT / I /

(She seems to retch but forces her hand to her mouth. She tries again.)

BABY / WANT / I /

(Again she retches, but less violently. PAPER watches with bemused fascination.)

Baby / want / I /

(Now BELL is unaffected. SIGN closes her eyes in profound despair. CALF pities SIGN. BELL looks to her, with a newly-discovered disdain.)

Is it harder now / or less hard / to die? /

SIGN: *(Opening her eyes at last.)* Believe me / in my heart / I wish you raped a thousand times /

(She turns to look at BELL .)

But that's my heart / and hearts are ignorant / my head says / she will make some wonder of it / oh / clever head /

it knows the length low cultures go to justify their animal existence / you'll be a legend / I see you on a coin / on a bank note / the will to live / the will to thrive / a thousand had her and she lived to 85 /

(For the first time, SIGN bursts out laughing. The sound, coming from her, is eerie and unexpected. SIGN lets it run its course, knowing full well laughter is a transgression. They watch her recover her poise.)

I laughed /

(She hangs her head, contrite.)

Oh /

(She moves her head on her neck, writhing.)

Oh / dear /

(She ceases the agonized movement. Her gaze meets the gaze of CALF.)

I laughed /

PAPER: *(Cruelly.)* Not a nice laugh /

SIGN: No /

PAPER: A coarse laugh /

SIGN: Yes /

PAPER: A laugh which / when we heard it / seemed worse than waving your arms /

(SIGN'S regard rests on CALF.)

Or walking naked down the street /

BELL: *(Gravely.)* Yes /

PAPER: That is how terrible it was /

BELL: Every bit as terrible / yes /

(Their indignation is less wounding to SIGN than her own sense of disgrace. She seems to attend on CALF's verdict.)

CALF: *(Without criticism.)* You are disappearing /

SIGN: Am I? /

CALF: You even / even you / are disappearing /

(SIGN takes measure of her verdict. Her mind loses none of its agility.)

SIGN: Either you love me / so powerfully love me / you wish me to become what you are / which is the way of lovers / is it not? / they cannot tolerate the slightest hint of difference / even the shadow of dissent /

(She regards them coolly.)

Or you are / all three of you / so deeply sunk in self-disgust you cannot bear to let me perish / knowing I will haunt the remnants of your compromised and /

CALF: Shh /

SIGN: SORDID LIFE /

CALF: Shh /

(CALF's tranquillity is too much for SIGN, who examining her with a distinct coolness, assesses her in CALF's own manner.)

SIGN: This disappearing / the very word / its so-soft syllables / its melancholy charm / we are disappearing / you say / as if nothing could be said or done / as if the sun set on your mother's garden / and a suffocating inertia slowed down your heart /

(SIGN is not vituperative.)

It's the genteel form of cowardice /

(She turns her face away, and stands.)

Now run /

BELL: Run? /

SIGN: Yes / now you have discovered the ecstasy of unhindered movement / why not run? / this paralysing etiquette / this starched and stiff formality / inflexible and / constrictive and / suffocating and / pull up your skirts and run / like a peasant / show your arse /

(She half-laughs.)

Oh dear / I laughed / twice now / my father would have frowned / as you leave send in the guard /

(She aches.)

My father / my father / my beloved father /

(She is defiant.)

THE GUARD NOW /

(The three women stand and are still for some time.)

CALF: A strange thing has taken place / imperceptible perhaps / your decision is scarcely any more to do with your history / or your people / is it? / it is to do with us / so deep is your loathing and contempt for us /

SIGN: Bottomless /

CALF: Yes / bottomless your contempt for us / and this compels you to an action which / I dare suggest / you would not / of your own free will / have persisted with / a pity / surely /

BELL: A pity /

PAPER: A pity / yes /

(SIGN seems to contemplate debating this and then renounces it.)

SIGN: You dared suggest /

(She turns her regard on CALF, who cannot hold her ground. Her own look falters. At once BELL piles from the room with a hiss of

106

clothing and panicked breath. This causes a scarcely-perceptible smile to flicker on SIGN'S lips.)

PAPER: *(On the verge of flight.)* We'll think of you /

SIGN: *(Further bemused by this.)* You will /

(SIGN'S tone hurts PAPER.)

PAPER: NOT ALWAYS SWEETLY /

SIGN: That's best /

PAPER: IF EVER / IF EVER SWEETLY /

(She glares.)

LONG LIVE THE NEW / THE NEW THINGS / SUNSHINE / BABIES / MEN / AND /

(The words jam in her mouth. She runs out. Almost at once she reappears, triumphant.)

THE GUARD'S GONE /

(PAPER leaves in a peal of laughter.)

SIGN: *(At last.)* To have your throat cut / like a wasp you said / a wasp inside your clothes / I liked that / so provide another / would you / equally apposite / to describe what it feels like to throw yourself out of a window? /

(CALF shrinks.)

Please /

(And closes her eyes in dismay.)

It helps /

(CALF is incapable of satisfying SIGN'S request. Instead, with a single hand, she creates a sign, one of terrible emptiness and finality. SIGN recognizes it and grasps the fullness of its meaning.)

A thousand years old is that sign / and whilst it wounds
me horribly / I am so happy to be admonished / and
abolished / by a gesture so perfectly made /

(CALF is utterly still.)

Only the greatest cultures know / how to make goodbye so
beautiful /

(She refines.)

The end of conversation / the start of death /

(CALF is enclosed.)

I'm going /

(CALF is impenetrable. SIGN half-leaves, but drags.)

My father gave that sign / less perfectly than you / on his
death-bed / I was so injured / injured because so much had
not been said / oh / so much unsaid / he knew / however
/ he knew /

(She reflects.)

And the sign includes the fact of this / intractable
frustration / I'm going / the sign says yes / but cease /
cease now /

(SIGN seems fixed.)

I am going /

(She fails to.)

Slowly /

(She cannot take her eyes from CALF's impervious immobility.)

Slowly / but I'm going /

(She studies harder. Her tranquillity deserts her.)

WE COME IN FOUR VERSIONS EVIDENTLY /
FOUR VERSIONS / ONE WILLING WHORE / ONE

WHO WHORES RELUCTANTLY / A SUICIDE /
THAT'S ME / AND THIS / THIS /

(She fathoms.)

You want to be killed / you want / I gasp / I gasp in
wonder / you want the shame of your killing to infect
their victory / a slow disease that claims / not them / but
the sons of their sons / so they writhe and drown in the
poisoned sink of their own history /

(SIGN marvels.)

I GASP /

(She adores.)

You are more proud / oh / vastly more proud /

(She half-smiles.)

MORE PROUD AND SAVAGE / than I could ever be /
You actually want / to be the subject of an atrocity /

(She leans closer to the immaculate form of CALF.)

Chill is your body /

(And closer.)

And your breath a frost /

(She exclaims.)

OH / I'D LOVE YOU / IF I BURST IN THIS ROOM /
AS THEY WILL / I'D LOVE AND MURDER YOU /

*(Nothing affects the frigidity of CALF. SIGN'S gaze sweeps her
adamantine surface. For a while they are similarly still, then SIGN
withdraws, inch by inch, as if from a wild but briefly placid animal.
After her departure is established, CALF's eyes open. She maintains
a perfect equanimity of appearance.)*

CALF: Wait for me /

(No sound comes.)

Wait for me /

(Her dread is not manifest in her features.)

I cannot do this on my own / this dying on my own / will someone / I'm going to be / going to be / someone / going to be / someone / oh someone / oh /

(One hand, placed across the other on her lap, rises and falls again.)

Someone /

(Her placidity is absolute.)

Someone /

*